THE BURNING LEG

Walking Scenes from Classic Fiction

THE BURNING LEG

Edited by Duncan Minshull

ET REMOTISSIMA PROPE

Published by Hesperus Press Limited
4 Rickett Street, London sw6 1ru
www.hesperuspress.com

First published by Hesperus Press Limited, 2010

Introduction © Duncan Minshull, 2010
Selection © Hesperus Press, 2010
Foreword © Will Self, 2010

'Bed 29', from *A Day in the Country and Other Stories* by Guy de Maupassant
translated by David Coward © David Coward 1990. Used by permission of
Oxford University Press.
'The Sudden Walk', from *Metamorphosis and Other Stories* by Franz Kafka,
translated by Michael Hoffman, © 2007 by Michael Hoffman. Used by
permission of Penguin, a division Penguin Group (USA) Inc.
English language translation, *A Nocturnal Expedition around my Room*
© Andrew Brown, 2004
English language translation, *Notes from the Underground* © Hugh Aplin, 2006

Designed and typeset by Fraser Muggeridge studio
Printed in Jordan by Jordan National Press

isbn: 978-1-84391-715-1

Contents

Foreword

I was raised to be a walker by my father. And when I say he was a walker, I mean 24-hour traverses of Dartmoor with only a few squares of chocolate and an apple for sustenance. Unfortunately, by the time I lolloped along he was a little too old for such extreme tramps, nevertheless our relationship was sealed during walks, especially after my parents separated – when I was nine – and my time with him was spent mostly *à pied*. There can be few people in this post-industrial age who have had this experience: a few years ago, visiting a friend who lives near Charmouth in Dorset, I stood on the celebrated and clayey cliffs, and thought not of their mother lode of fossils – which kick-started the scientific revolution of the nineteenth century – but that the last time I had been on this coast, I had walked there from Taunton with my father.

It was a seventy mile walk and I don't remember a great deal about it save for one evening we spent in a rural pub with a group of holidaying miners. My father had a great contempt for licensing laws and on this occasion he let me have several half-pints of cider – I must have been twelve or thirteen. He also debated with the miners: the whys and wherefores of the then government's prices and incomes policy, the role of union power generally, and towards midnight (there was a lock-in), they'd got on to the social contract and Jean-Jacques Rousseau.

It was Rousseau, a great walker, who observed that we think at walking pace; and while I went on to have a perfectly troubled relationship with my father, in the decade since his death I have come to prize his legacy, which was this: all those thoughts divulged at walking pace; the steady 4/4 beat of his metre as he read the landscape then interpreted it for me. The Australian aboriginals believe that the primordial ancestors of all the fauna on their vast and sun-baked island continent walked there across the Arafura Sea, and then headed inland, singing up mangrove swamps, mountains and deserts as they went. If it isn't too fanciful, I'd like to suggest that my own father – an academic who specialised in theories of urban and regional planning – was engaging in his own 'singing up' of the country, as we walked across England and Wales.

Then latterly Australia itself, where he emigrated in 1980. Some of my last walks with my father were in the hills along the Mudgee River, or else at the Tidbinbilla nature reserve – both within an hour's drive of his home in Canberra. Since his death the impulse I've always had to walk – but which was hobbled by the fetters of grosser housebound pleasures – has grown irresistible. It began conventionally enough with picturesque ascents in the Scottish hills and rambles along the Suffolk coast, yet soon enough I felt frogmarched towards a different kind of walking: an anti-Romantic pursuit of the sublime, not in nature, but in those portions of civilisation that are awesomely unregarded.

So it is that for the past six years, each summer, I have walked out from my home in South London along one of the cardinal compass lines: north then north-west, south then south-east – and so on. I have become fixated on the hinterland of the city – only closely observable on foot – that other travellers simply leap over by train and car. I have delighted in the curious oxbows of farmland left marooned by the course of fluvial motorways, and felt like an insurgent, tiptoeing along bramble-lined paths through a landscape devoid of people – until, that is, I reached a road.

I have had one companion on these walks – and that's been my father's sensibility. Indeed, the consistency with which he has walked beside me, invisible, has verged on the Eliotic; and while I said that the idea of him 'singing up' the country like an Aboriginal spirit seemed a little fanciful when he was alive, now that he's long dead it has become indisputable: fathers and sons, mothers and daughters – we walk our way through life hand-in-hand, and experience itself remains inchoate until we have discussed it.

The Burning Leg is like a portable houseful of fathers and mothers, each of its extracts a 'singing up' of another country and another time. As I say, I walk a great deal – and I read a great deal as well, yet the two are often difficult to combine successfully: the prose narrative undercutting rather than counterpointing the story of the walk itself; all too often, stopping to read a book when you're walking feels like reading parallel texts. This book, then, is the solution, for each of the pieces is short enough to be devoured along with a few squares of chocolate and an apple; while since all of them are concerned with the business afoot, there need be no jibing. Who knows, perhaps if you keep going with both *The Burning Leg* and your own, two muscular ones, you'll make it across Dartmoor by this time tomorrow.

– Will Self, 2010

Introduction

Walkers have often wandered across the page. But accompanying their early efforts doesn't reveal much about this simple and complex activity. In the Bible, say, or in various epics, mythology and folklore, people are named as walkers and that's usually it – end of journey, end of story. Other journeys have allegorical meaning, where the road ahead, stretching to the horizon and full of hardship, reflects the course of one's own travels through life: 'Prepare to take The Road of Life,' and so forth. Yet whoever went early – be it Christ through the wilderness, Xenophon's marching men, Dante's 'roamer of the realms' – went without any examination. How, then, can readers appreciate the whys and wherefores of going on foot?

The conciseness and intimacy of the essay form helps. Its heyday was Victorian and Edwardian. It was used by author-walkers such as Robert Louis Stevenson, Leslie Stephen and his daughter Virginia Woolf to describe rural and urban routes well trod and, more usefully, to delve into the physical, psychological and spiritual reasons for setting out. You'll get some knicker-bockered bluster about what clothes to wear, the right boots, the right gait, and this can be skipped if too loud. Then, time-wise before and after the essayists, comes another type with insight – the poet-walkers. Among them are John Gay, John Clare and Edward Thomas, who record what it means (and feels) to put one foot in front of the other. Lots of poets walk to beat out a meter for their lines, and through the voices of their verses you can sense the rhythms of a journey just made.

But pedestrian literature needn't stop here. Another group moves across the page, and it is steered into *The Burning Leg*. Walkers in novels and stories are placed on path, peak and street for the same reasons that preoccupy essayists and poets. Except, these walkers being fictional creations, their motivations are imbued with more dash and drama. After one of his habitual hikes across London, Charles Dickens said, 'Something always happens on taking a walk' – which is very true. The road is a stage. The road offers possibility. The world comes closer now. And perhaps Dickens wasn't only referring to his own wanderings. He was suggesting to us: look how I can toy with the destinies of Oliver Twist and Little Dorrit, who are always out there, footing it.

But before Dickens and Co., what of earlier pedestrians? There is Parson Adams, for instance. Put on an olde Englishe road by Henry Fielding to enjoy himself, he soon outdoes his carriage-bound friends with cries of 'Aye, Aye, Catch Me If You Can' and heads for a grassy speck to wait. How good it was – still is – to snub the wheel. How good also to see and feel 'the turf'; and his communing with nature echoes likeminded souls found in the novels of George Eliot, Leo Tolstoy, D.H. Lawrence. Though by the time Mark Twain sends a couple of over-packed trekkers up a track to see a sunset, we might think rural rambling goes too far. Thankfully high peaks and high comedy offer a welcome corrective.

Then in Edith Wharton's *The Reef*, a figure strolls through Paris as if strolling through some lovely meadow with the Parson. For the sights and sounds that waylay George Darrow do so in bucolic fashion: he is at one with old bridges and old buildings. He is free to relax and reminisce, sink slowly back in time. But imagine if his footsteps were to segue into the London of Edgar Allan Poe... what a shock of the Victorian new would hit! From street level we follow a modern city in motion, with its familiar realities and paradoxes. Poe's people move 'like a tide', yet with 'knitted brows', vital and anxious. Pavements are accessible, yet cracked and clogged; well lit, yet swathed in darkness. There is a sense of dislocation here that would defeat Darrow and it's caught in the way everyone walks. Though they don't walk. They bobble to and fro, jostle, bustle and reel. And from this tumult in Poe's story 'The Man of the Crowd' comes a classic figure – the flâneur. An indifferent meanderer, an observer of the scene, he leaves his café and newspaper behind to botanize on the asphalt. Amongst all these people, he is alone in life.

Loners fascinate on the fictional road, which might have something to do with snobbery and fear. Since the emergence of the novel only the poor and the criminal, and perhaps a poet or two beating out that meter, have had reason not to travel by horse, coach or mechanised carriage. Many dedicated walkers, especially single, are viewed as infra dig. Even suspicious. When William Congreve's Millamant, a dissenter ahead, says in *The Way of the World*, 'I nauseate walking,' she could be saying, 'I nauseate walkers,' too, and speaks for many of her age and later. This of course gives writers tremendous scope, for they can turn these maligned types into memorable characters. Here for instance comes the Outsider: think of the Thomas Hardy novels that open with a stranger passing through. Here comes the Outcast: Elizabeth Gaskell's Esther paces the pavements alone. And all those eccentrics, with their singular ambitions reflected in solitary journeys – one is 'mesmerised' by a mountain peak and one will 'hike' across his bed-chamber as if it's the great beyond. They are restless souls *in extremis*, seeking some relief after setting off.

Another burning leg belongs to Elizabeth Bennett, who seeks relief from the confines of the drawing room, and the gossip. Outdoors she gets muddy and 'glows' – Austen's way of making her different to other women in *Pride and Prejudice*. More importantly, her excursions *with* somebody, with Darcy, will at last bring awareness – 'Why is he so altered?' Writers use the aura of the loner; they also use social walks to get characters together and sort out their destinies. From the faintly suggestive *passeggiatas* described in Henry James to the highly charged strolls in D.H. Lawrence, it's all happening. People walk and talk, and events take a turn. Later they take their own children out, and the ritual goes on.

Soon the light fades. And others start out. If the road is a stage, then the nightwalkers invite everything to happen. Under artificial light, under the vagaries of gas-light rather than electric, the city changes. Meanwhile, the countryside is plunged into black, illumined by the moon and the stars, which have similar powers of transformation. Gerald and Gudrun in *Women in Love* might relish the dark of lovers' lane, but for many such nocturnal excursions will end badly as melodrama and Grand Guignol take over. Dangers are made real or are projected by the individual. How else can it be for Cossette in *Les Misérables*? How – we ask – can Victor Hugo even do this, put a child on the road without a moon for company? She counts aloud to fortify her steps and somewhere she hopes – we hope – 'a lighted candle' shines. We also recall that scene in *Villette*, when 'moustachioed men' loiter close. How, too, can Charlotte Brontë put a young woman in a foreign town, off the boulevard, after dusk? But the truly dreadful nightwalk is young Goodman Brown's, courtesy of Nathaniel Hawthorne, who fuses the external dangers of walking at night ('oh, that dark clad company') with inner dread ('the despair, the frenzy') – and does so brilliantly. It will stop you in your tracks. It will send Gerald and Gudrun home, too.

But back to those early accounts. No, they don't examine why people walk; nor do they tell us *how* people walk. People just... walked. Yet novels and stories give us more. They show that identity is bound up with movement, and a character's gait says much about them, which can be funny and poignant. Father Brown ponders the sound of footsteps near his room, before deciding they belong to a dubious sort. On a Maupassant stroll the women trail their skirts, the soldiers drag their sabres, ah yes – we get the symbolism there. Just as Hardy sends Mrs Yeobright to find her son, only for a stranger's stride to change everything as she notes 'the peculiarities of his walk'. And a tramp in Richard Middleton's tale realises he is new to the role after hearing, 'I could tell by the way you walk. Perhaps you expect something at the other end. You'll grow out of that.'

And writers find choice words for catching movement. 'Stamp!' is rather wonderful when used by Katherine Mansfield to show how Kezia tackles a stile, and after she succeeds we know she'll stamp her way through life, too. Poe, as mentioned, sums up city congestion with a limited choice, whereas Twain's Grand Tourers exalt in the Swiss air and make their ways expansively. Pushing and plunging, striding and swinging, loping, loafing and hurrying, and when desperate – slopping and clawing. Expansive yes, but it adds to a growing sense of parody – of two Americans in the Old World, two men small in the face of Nature. And whilst on the subject: where does that 'burning leg' come from?

One of the final journeys is made by a man and a dog along a snow-bound trail. It's such a familiar duo, it's surprising they haven't shown up more often. Except the man isn't very interesting. There are no compelling reasons for starting out, no affinity with nature or bond with his four-legged friend. Only the need to make camp before nightfall, otherwise the cold might kill him. So suspense mounts in Jack London's story as we watch the man push on, with few words enriching the way he moves – just 'plunging'. In fact, he could have come from one of the early accounts, lacking as he does any appreciation of his actions or any psychological depth. What a way to sign off! But in between, here's hoping the nature lovers and city types, the loners and couples, the nightwalkers and oddbods have enough in them to prove Dickens right. That something always happens on a walk, either in the head or on the road ahead. I hope you enjoy following them all.

– Duncan Minshull, 2010

Editor's Note

Most of the following novel extracts, short stories and stage fragments are taken from a period that covers three hundred years, from the 1700s to the 1920s. Many of the British extracts come from walking heydays – from the Romantic, Victorian and Edwardian eras – when characters roamed open-plan fields, enclosed fields, parks and gardens and a burgeoning urban scene, especially after industrialisation. There are also walkers out of Europe, Russia, New Zealand and America. And their excursions are intended to show where they went and why they went, in roughly chronological order. The burning leg of the title is Willoughby's leg from *The Egoist* by George Meredith. In a 'cavalier court-suit trouser' it often excited the ladies. I use it to suggest passion as well – the passion for setting off.

THE BURNING LEG

Walking Scenes from Classic Fiction

For June Minshull, who's always on the move...

I am looking for something more mysterious. For the path you read about in books, the old lane choked with undergrowth, whose entrance the weary prince could not discover.

Alain-Fournier

All Before Them

In either hand the hastening Angel caught
Our lingering parents, and to the eastern gate
Led them direct, and down the cliff as fast
To the subjected plain; then disappeared.
They, looking back, all the eastern side beheld
Of Paradise, so late their happy seat,
Waved over by that flaming brand; the gate
With dreadful faces thronged, and fiery arms:
Some natural tears they dropt, but wiped them soon;
The world was all before them, where to choose
Their place of rest, and Providence their guide.
They, hand in hand, with wandering steps and slow,
Through Eden took their solitary way.

John Milton, *Paradise Lost* (1667)

Gardens

A smooth lawn lay before you, dotted with groups of rhododendrons, which grew in more perfection here than anywhere else in the county. To the right there were the kitchen gardens, the fish-pond, and an orchard bordered by a dry moat, and a broken ruin of a wall, in some places thicker than it was high, and everywhere overgrown with trailing ivy, yellow stonecrop, and dark moss. To the left there was a broad gravelled walk, down which, years ago, when the place had been a convent, the quiet nuns had walked hand in hand; a wall bordered with espaliers, and shadowed on one side by goodly oaks, which shut out the flat landscape, and circled in the house and gardens with a darkening shelter.

Mary Elizabeth Braddon, *Lady Audley's Secret* (1862)

Meadows Green

Their way lay just above the bank of this river. Here, therefore, Christian and his companion walked with great delight. They drank of the water of the river, which was pleasant and enlivening to their weary spirits. Besides, on the banks of this river, on either side, were green trees with all manner of fruit; and the leaves they ate to prevent surfeits and other diseases incident to those that heat their blood by travel. On either side of the river was also a meadow, curiously beautified with lilies; and it was green all the year long. In this meadow they lay down and slept, for here they might lie down safely. When they awoke, they gathered again of the fruit of the trees and drank again of the water of the river, and then lay down again to sleep. Thus they did several days and nights. Then they sang:

> *Behold ye how these crystal streams do glide,*
> *To comfort pilgrims by the highway side!*
> *The meadows green, besides their fragrant smell,*
> *Yield dainties for them; and he who can tell*
> *What pleasant fruit, yea, leaves, these trees do yield,*
> *Will soon sell all, that he may buy this field.*

So when they were disposed to go on (for they were not as yet at their journey's end) they ate and drank and departed.

John Bunyan, *The Pilgrim's Progress* (1678)

Nearly to the Top?

The Rigi-Kulm is an imposing Alpine mass, six thousand feet high, which stands by itself, and commands a mighty prospect of blue lakes, green valleys, and snowy mountains – a compact and magnificent picture three hundred miles in circumference.

The ascent is made by rail, or horseback, or on foot, as one may prefer. I and my agent panoplied ourselves in walking costume, one bright morning, and started down the lake on the steamboat. We got ashore at the village of Wäggis; three quarters of an hour distant from Lucerne. This village is at the foot of the mountain.

We were soon tramping leisurely up the leafy mule-path, and then the talk began to flow, as usual. It was twelve o'clock noon, and a breezy, cloudless day; the ascent was gradual, and the glimpses, from under the curtaining boughs, of blue water, and tiny sailboats, and beetling cliffs, were as charming as glimpses of dreamland. All the circumstances were perfect – and the anticipations, too, for we should soon be enjoying, for the first time, that wonderful spectacle, an Alpine sunrise – the object of our journey. There was (apparently) no real need to hurry, for the guidebook made the walking distance from Wäggis to the summit only three hours and a quarter. I say 'apparently', because the guidebook had already fooled us once – about the distance from Allerheiligen to Oppenau – and for aught I knew it might be getting ready to fool us again. We were only certain as to the altitudes – we calculated to find out for ourselves how many hours it is from the bottom to the top. The summit is six thousand feet above the sea, but only forty-five hundred feet above the lake. When we had walked half an hour, we were fairly into the swing and humor of the under-taking, so we cleared for action; that is to say, we got a boy whom we met to carry our alpenstocks and satchels and overcoats and things for us; that left us free for business.

I suppose we must have stopped oftener to stretch out on the grass in the shade and take a bit of a smoke than this boy was used to, for presently he asked if it had been our idea to hire him by the job, or by the year? We told him he could move along if he was in a hurry. He said he wasn't in such a very particular hurry, but he wanted to get to the top while he was young. We told him to clear out, then, and leave the things at the uppermost hotel and say we should be along presently. He said he would secure us a hotel if he could, but if they were all full he would ask them to build another one and hurry up and get the paint and plaster dry against we arrived. Still gently chaffing us, he pushed ahead, up the trail, and soon disappeared.

By six o'clock we were pretty high up in the air, and the view of lake and mountains had greatly grown in breadth and interest. We halted awhile at a little public house, where we had bread and cheese and a quart or two of fresh milk, out on the porch, with the big panorama all before us – and then moved on again.

Ten minutes afterward we met a hot, red-faced man plunging down the mountain, with mighty strides, swinging his alpenstock ahead of him, and taking a grip on the ground with its iron point to support these big strides. He stopped, fanned himself with his hat, swabbed the perspiration from his face and neck with a red handkerchief, panted a moment or two, and asked how far it was to Wäggis. I said three hours. He looked surprised, and said, 'Why, it seems as if I could toss a biscuit into the lake from here, it's so close by. Is that an inn, there?'

I said it was.

'Well,' said he, 'I can't stand another three hours, I've had enough today; I'll take a bed there.'

I asked, 'Are we nearly to the top?'

'Nearly to the *top*! Why, bless your soul, you haven't really started, yet.'

I said we would put up at the inn, too. So we turned back and ordered a hot supper, and had quite a jolly evening of it with this Englishman.

The German landlady gave us neat rooms and nice beds, and when I and my agent turned in, it was with the resolution to be up early and make the utmost of our first Alpine sunrise. But of course we were dead tired, and slept like policemen; so when we awoke in the morning and ran to the window it was already too late, because it was half past eleven. It was a sharp disappointment. However, we ordered breakfast and told the landlady to call the Englishman, but she said he was already up and off at daybreak – and swearing mad about something or other. We could not find out what the matter was. He had asked the land-lady the altitude of her place above the level of the lake, and she told him fourteen hundred and ninety-five feet. That was all that was said; then he lost his temper. He said that between — fools and guidebooks, a man could acquire ignorance enough in twenty-four hours in a country like this to last him a year. Harris believed our boy had been loading him up with misinformation; and this was probably the case, for his epithet described that boy to a dot.

We got under way about the turn of noon, and pulled out for the summit again, with a fresh and vigorous step… In the course of a couple of hours we reached a fine breezy altitude where the little shepherd huts had big stones all over their roofs to hold them down to the earth when the great storms rage. The country was wild and rocky about here, but there were plenty of trees, plenty of moss, and grass…

Presently we came upon half a dozen sheep nibbling grass in the spray of a stream of clear water that sprang from a rock wall a hundred feet high, and all at once our ears were startled with a melodious 'Lul… l… l… lul-lul-*la*hee-o-o-o!' pealing joyously from a near but invisible source, and recognized that we were hearing for the first time the famous Alpine *jodel* in its own native wilds. And we recognized, also, that it was that sort of quaint commingling of baritone and falsetto which at home we call 'Tyrolese warbling'.

The jodeling (pronounced *yo*dling – emphasis on the o) con-tinued, and was very pleasant and inspiriting to hear. Now the jodeler appeared – a shepherd boy of sixteen – and in our glad-ness and gratitude we gave him a franc to jodel some more. So he jodeled and we listened. We moved on, presently, and he generously jodeled us out of sight. After about fifteen minutes we came across another shepherd boy who was jodeling, and gave him half a franc to keep it up. He also jodeled us out of sight. After that, we found a jodeler every ten minutes. We gave the first one eight cents, the second one six cents, the third one four, the fourth one a penny, contributed nothing to Nos. 5, 6, and 7, and during the remainder of the day hired the rest of the jodelers, at a franc apiece, not to jodel any more. There is somewhat too much of this jodeling in the Alps.

About the middle of the afternoon we passed through a prodigious natural gateway called the Felsenthor, formed by two enormous upright rocks, with a third lying across the top. There was a very attractive little hotel close by, but our energies were not conquered yet, so we went on.

Three hours afterward we came to the railway track. It was planted straight up the mountain with the slant of a ladder that leans against a house, and it seemed to us that man would need good nerves who proposed to travel up it or down it either...

At ten minutes past six we reached the Kaltbad station, where there is a spacious hotel with great verandas which command a majestic expanse of lake and mountain scenery. We were pretty well fagged out, now, but as we did not wish to miss the Alpine sunrise, we got through our dinner as quickly as possible and hurried off to bed. It was unspeakably comfortable to stretch our weary limbs between the cool, damp sheets. And how we did sleep! – for there is no opiate like Alpine pedestrianism.

In the morning we both awoke and leaped out of bed at the same instant and ran and stripped aside the window curtains. But we suffered a bitter disappointment again: it was already half past three in the afternoon.

We dressed sullenly and in ill spirits, each accusing the other of over-sleeping. Harris said if we had brought the courier along, as we ought to have done, we should not have missed these sunrises. I said he knew very well that one of us would have had to sit up and wake the courier; and I added that we were having trouble enough to take care of ourselves, on this climb, without having to take care of a courier besides.

During breakfast our spirits came up a little, since we found by the guidebook that in the hotels on the summit the tourist is not left to trust to luck for his sunrise, but is roused betimes by a man who goes through the halls with a great Alpine horn, blowing blasts that would raise the dead. And there was another consoling thing: the guidebook said that up there on the summit the guests did not wait to dress much, but seized a red bed-blanket and sailed out arrayed like an Indian. This was good; this would be romantic; two hundred and fifty people grouped on the windy summit, with their hair flying and their red blankets flapping, in the solemn presence of the snowy ranges and the messenger splendors and the coming sun, would be a striking and memorable spectacle. So it was good luck, not ill luck, that we had missed those other sunrises.

We were informed by the guidebook that we were now 3,228 feet above the level of the lake – therefore full two-thirds of our journey had been accomplished. We got away at a quarter past four p.m...

We climbed and climbed; and we kept on climbing. We reached about forty summits, but there was always another one just ahead. It came on to rain, and it rained in dead earnest. We were soaked through and it was bitter cold. Next a smoky fog of clouds covered the whole region densely, and we took to the railway ties to keep from getting lost. Sometimes we slopped along in a narrow path on the left hand side of the track, but by and by when the fog blew aside a little and we saw that we were treading the rampart of a precipice and that our left elbows were projecting over a perfectly boundless and bottomless vacancy, we gasped, and jumped for the ties again.

The night shut down, dark and drizzly and cold. About eight in the evening the fog lifted and showed us a well-worn path which led up a very steep rise to the left. We took it, and as soon as we had got far enough from the railway to render the finding it again an impossibility, the fog shut down on us once more.

We were in a bleak, unsheltered place, now, and had to trudge right along, in order to keep warm, though we rather expected to go over a precipice sooner or later. About nine o'clock we made an important discovery – that we were not in any path. We groped around a while on our hands and knees, but we could not find it; so we sat down in the mud and the wet scant grass to wait. We were terrified into this by being suddenly confronted with a vast body which showed itself vaguely for an instant and in the next instant was smothered in the fog again. It was really the hotel we were after, monstrously magnified by the fog, but we took it for the face of a precipice, and decided not to try to claw up it.

We sat there an hour, with chattering teeth and quivering bodies, and quarreled over all sorts of trifles, but gave most of our attention to abusing each other for the stupidity of deserting the railway track. We sat with our backs to the precipice, because what little wind there was came from that quarter. At some time or other the fog thinned a little; we did not know when, for we were facing the empty universe and the thinness could not show; but at last Harris happened to look around, and there stood a huge, dim, spectral hotel where the precipice had been. One could faintly discern the windows and chimneys, and a dull blur of lights. Our first emotion was deep, unutterable gratitude, our next was a foolish rage, born of the suspicion that possibly the hotel had been visible three-quarters of an hour while we sat there in those cold puddles quarreling.

Yes, it was the Rigi-Kulm hotel – the one that occupies the extreme summit, and whose remote little sparkle of lights we had often seen glinting high aloft among the stars from our balcony away down yonder in Lucerne. The crusty portier and the crusty clerks gave us the surly reception which their kind deal out in prosperous times, but by mollifying them with an extra display of obsequiousness and servility we finally got them to show us to the room which our boy had engaged for us.

We got into some dry clothing, and while our supper was preparing we loafed forsakenly through a couple of vast cavernous drawing-rooms, one of which had a stove in it. This stove was in a corner, and densely walled around with people. There were some Americans and some Germans, but one could see that the great majority were English.

We lounged into an apartment where there was a great crowd, to see what was going on. It was a memento-magazine. The tourists were eagerly buying all sorts and styles of paper-cutters, marked 'Souvenir of the Rigi', with handles made of the little curved horn of the ostensible chamois; there were all manner of wooden goblets and such things, similarly marked. I was going to buy a paper-cutter, but I believed I could remember the cold comfort of the Rigi-Kulm without it, so I smothered the impulse.

Supper warmed us, and we went immediately to bed – but first, as Mr Baedeker requests all tourists to call his attention to any errors which they may find in his guidebooks, I dropped him a line to inform him that when he said the foot journey from Wäggis to the summit was only three hours and a quarter, he missed it by just about three days…

We curled up in the clammy beds, and went to sleep without rocking. We were so sodden with fatigue that we never stirred nor turned over till the blooming blasts of the Alpine horn aroused us. It may well be imagined that we did not lose any time. We snatched on a few odds and ends of clothing, cocooned ourselves in the proper red blankets, and plunged along the halls and out into the whistling wind bareheaded. We saw a tall wooden scaffolding on the very peak of the summit, a hundred yards away, and made for it. We rushed up the stairs to the top of this scaffolding, and stood there, above the vast outlying world, with hair flying and ruddy blankets waving and cracking in the fierce breeze.

'Fifteen minutes too late, at last!' said Harris, in a vexed voice. 'The sun is clear above the horizon.'

'No matter,' I said, 'it is a most magnificent spectacle, and we will see it do the rest of its rising anyway.'

In a moment we were deeply absorbed in the marvel before us, and dead to everything else. The great cloud-barred disk of the sun stood just above a limitless expanse of tossing white-caps – so to speak – a billowy chaos of massy mountain domes and peaks draped in imperishable snow, and flooded with an opaline glory of changing and dissolving splendors…

We could not speak. We could hardly breathe. We could only gaze in drunken ecstasy and drink it in. Presently Harris exclaimed, 'Why –nation, it's going *down*!'

Perfectly true. We had missed the *morning* hornblow, and slept all day. This was stupefying. Harris said, 'Look here, the sun isn't the spectacle – it's *us* – stacked up here on top of this gallows, in these idiotic blankets, and two hundred and fifty well-dressed men and women down here gawking up at us and not caring a straw whether the sun rises or sets, as long as they've got such a ridiculous spectacle as this to set down in their memorandum-books. They seem to be laughing their ribs loose, and there's one girl there that appears to be going all to pieces. I never saw such a man as you before. I think you are the very last possibility in the way of an ass.'

'What have *I* done?' I answered, with heat.

'What have you done? You've got up at half past seven o'clock in the evening to see the sun rise, that's what you've done.'

'And have you done any better, I'd like to know? I always used to get up with the lark, till I came under the petrifying influence of your turgid intellect.'

'*You* used to get up with the lark – oh, no doubt – you'll get up with the hangman one of these days. But you ought to be ashamed to be jawing here like this, in a red blanket, on a forty-foot scaffold on top of the Alps.'

And so the customary quarrel went on. When the sun was fairly down, we slipped back to the hotel in the charitable gloaming, and went to bed again. We had encountered the horn-blower on the way, and he had tried to collect compensation, not only for announcing the sunset, which we did see, but for the sunrise, which we had totally missed. But we said no, we only took our solar rations on the 'European plan' – pay for what you get. He promised to make us hear his horn in the morning, if we were alive.

Mark Twain, 'The Rigi-Kulm' (1880)

Nearly to the Top too

On the brown of a pine-plumed hillock there sat a little man with his back against a tree. A venerable pipe hung from his mouth and smoke-wreaths curled slowly skyward. He was muttering to himself with his eyes fixed on an irregular black opening in the green wall of forest at the foot of the hill. Two vague wagon-ruts led into the shadows.

The little man took his pipe in his hands and addressed the listening pines.

'I wonder what the devil it leads to,' said he.

A grey, fat rabbit came lazily from a thicket and sat in the opening. Softly stroking his stomach with his paw, he looked at the little man in a thoughtful manner. The little man threw a stone, and the rabbit blinked and ran through an opening. Green, shadowy portals seemed to closed behind him.

The little man started. 'He's gone down that roadway,' he said with ecstatic mystery to the pines. He sat a long time and contemplated the door to the forest. Finally, he arose, and awakening his limbs, started away. But he stopped and looked back.

'I can't imagine what it leads to,' muttered he. He trudged over the brown mats of pin needles, to where, in a fringe of laurel, a tent was pitched, and merry flames caroused about some logs. A pudgy man was fuming over a collection of tin dishes. He came forward and waved a plate furiously in the little man's face.

'I've washed the dishes for three days. What do you think I am –'

He ended a red oration with a roar, 'Damned if I do it any more.'

The little man gazed dim-eyes away. 'I've been wonderin' what it leads to.'

'What?'

'That road out yonder. I've been wonderin' what it leads to. Maybe, some discovery or something.'

The pudgy man laughed. 'You're an idiot. It leads to ol' Jim Boy's over on the Lumberland Pike.'

'Ho!' said the little man, 'I don't believe that.'

The pudgy man swore. 'Fool, what does it lead to, then?'

'I don't know just what, but I'm sure it leads to something great or something. It looks like it.'

While the pudgy man was cursing, two more men came from obscurity with fish dangling from birch twigs. The pudgy man made an obviously Herculean struggle and a meal was prepared. As he was drinking his cup of coffee, he suddenly spilled it and swore. The little man was wandering off.

'He's gone to look at that hole,' cried the pudgy man.

The little man went to the edge of the pine-plumed hillock and, sitting down, began to make smoke and regard the door to the forest. There was stillness for an hour. Compact clouds hung unstirred in the sky. The pines stood motionless, and pondering.

Suddenly, the little man slapped his knees and bit his tongue. He stood up and determinedly filled his pipe, rolling his eye over the bowl to the doorway. Keeping his eyes fixed he slid dangerously to the foot of the hillock and walked down the wagon-ruts. A moment later, he passed from the noise of the sunshine to the gloom of the woods.

The green portals closed, shutting out things. The little man trudged on alone.

Tall tangled grass grew in the roadway, and the trees bended obstructing branches. The little man followed over pine-clothed ridges and down through water-soaked swales. His shoes were cut by rocks of the mountains and he sank ankle-deep in mud and moss of swamps. A curve, just ahead, lured him miles.

Finally, as he wended the side of a ridge, the road disappeared from beneath his feet. He battled with hordes of ignorant bushes on his way to knolls and solitary trees which invited him. Once he came to a tall, bearded pine. He climbed it, and perceived in the distance a peak. He uttered an ejaculation and fell out.

He scrambled to his feet. 'That's Jones's Mountain, I guess. It's about six miles from our camp as the crow flies.'

He changed his course away from the mountain and attacked the bushes again. He climbed over great logs, golden-brown in decay, and was opposed by thickets of dark green laurel. A brook slid through the ooze of a swamp, cedars and hemlocks hung their spray to the edges of pools.

The little man began to stagger in his walk. After a time he stopped and mopped his brow.

'My legs are about to shrivel up and drop off,' he said… 'Still, if I keep on in this direction, I am safe to strike the Lumberland Pike before sundown.'

He dived at a clump of tag-alders, and emerging, confronted Jones's Mountain.

The wanderer sat down in a clear space and fixed his eyes on the summit. His mouth opened widely, and his body swayed at times. The little man and the peak stared in silence.

A lake lay near the foot of the mountain. In its bed of water-grass some frogs leered at the sky and crooned. The sun sank in red silence and the shadows of the pines grew formidable. The expectant hush of evening fell upon the peak and the little man.

A leaping pickerel off on the water created a silver circle that was lost in black shadows. The little man shook himself and started to his feet, crying, 'For the love of Mike, there's eyes in this mountain! I feel 'em! Eyes!'

He fell on his face.

When he looked again, he immediately sprang erect and ran. 'It's comin'!'

The mountain was approaching.

The little man scurried sobbing through the thick growth. He felt his brain turning to water. He vanquished brambles with mighty bounds.

But after a time he came again to the foot of the mountain.

'God!' he howled, 'it's been follerin' me.' He groveled. Casting his eyes upward made circles swirl in his blood. 'I'm shackled

I guess.' As he felt the heel of the mountain about to crush his head, he sprang again to his feet. He grasped a handful of small stones and hurled them.

'Damn you!' he shrieked, loudly. The pebbles rang against the face of the mountain.

The little man then made an attack. He climbed with his hands and feet, wildly. Brambles forced him back and stones slid beneath his feet. The peak swayed and tottered and was about to smite with a granite arm. The summit was a blaze of red wrath.

But the little man at last reached the top. He swaggered with valor to the edge of the cliff.

His hands were scornfully in his pockets.

He gazed at the western horizon edged sharply against a yellow sky. 'Ho!' he said. 'There's Boyd's house and the Lumber-land Pike.'

The mountain under his feet was motionless.

Stephen Crane, 'The Mesmeric Mountain' (1902)

All Roads Lead to...

Oliver reached the stile at which the by-path terminated; and once more gained the high-road. It was eight o'clock now; and, though he was nearly five miles away from the town, he ran, and hid behind the hedges, by turns, till noon, fearing that he might be pursued and overtaken. Then he sat down to rest by the side of a milestone, and began to think, for the first time, where he had better go and try to live.

The stone by which he was seated, bore in large characters an intimation that it was just seventy miles from that spot to London. The name awakened a new train of ideas in the boy's mind. London! – that great large place! – nobody – not even Mr Bumble – could ever find him there! He had often heard the old men in the workhouse, too, say that no lad of spirit need want in London; and that there were ways of living in that vast city, which those who had been bred up in country parts had no idea of. It was the very place for a homeless boy, who must die in the streets unless someone helped him. As these things passed through his thoughts, he jumped upon his feet, and again walked forward.

He had diminished the distance between himself and London by full four miles more, before he recollected how much he must undergo ere he could hope to reach his place of destination. As this consideration forced itself upon him, he slackened his pace a little, and meditated upon his means of getting there. He had a crust of bread, a coarse shirt, and two pairs of stockings in his bundle. He had a penny too – a gift of Sowerberry's after some funeral in which he had acquitted himself more than ordinarily well – in his pocket. 'A clean shirt,' thought Oliver, 'is a very comfortable thing – very; and so are two pairs of darned stockings; and so is a penny; but they are small helps to a sixty-five miles' walk in winter time.'... so, after a good deal of thinking to no particular purpose, he changed his little bundle over to the other shoulder, and trudged on.

Oliver walked twenty miles that day; and all that time tasted nothing but the crust of dry bread, and a few draughts of water, which he begged at the cottage-doors by the roadside. When the night came, he turned in to a meadow; and, creeping close under a hay-rick, determined to lie there till morning. He felt frightened at first, for the wind moaned dismally over the empty fields: and he was cold and hungry, and more alone than he had ever felt before. Being very tired with his walk, however, he soon fell asleep and forgot his troubles.

He felt cold and stiff when he got up next morning, and so hungry that he was obliged to exchange the penny for a small loaf in the very first village through which he passed. He had walked no more than twelve miles, when night closed in again. His feet were sore, and his legs so weak that they trembled beneath him. Another night passed in the bleak damp air only made him worse; and, when he set forward on his journey next morning, he could hardly crawl along.

He waited at the bottom of a steep hill till a stagecoach came up, and then begged of the outside passengers; but there were very few who took any notice of him, and even those told him to wait till they got to the top of the hill, and then let them see how far he could run for a halfpenny. Poor Oliver tried to keep up with the coach a little way, but was unable to do it, by reason of his fatigue and sore feet. When the outsiders saw this, they put their halfpence back into their pockets again, declaring that he was an idle young dog, and didn't deserve anything; and the coach rattled away and left only a cloud of dust behind.

In some villages, large painted boards were fixed up: warning all persons who begged within the district that they would be sent to jail. This frightened Oliver very much, and made him glad to get out of those villages with all possible expedition. In others, he would stand about the inn-yards, and look mournfully at every one who passed: a proceeding which generally terminated in the landlady's ordering one of the post-boys who were lounging about, to drive that strange boy out of the place, for she was sure he had come to steal something...

In fact, if it had not been for a good-hearted turnpike-man, and a benevolent old lady, Oliver's troubles would have been shortened by the very same process which put an end to his mother's; in other words, he would most assuredly have fallen dead upon the king's highway. But the turnpike-man gave him a meal of bread and cheese; and the old lady, who had a ship-wrecked grandson wandering bare-footed in some distant part of the earth, took pity upon the poor orphan, and gave him what little she could afford – and more...

Early on the seventh morning after he had left his native place, Oliver limped slowly into the little town of Barnet. The window-shutters were closed, the street was empty, not a soul had awakened to the business of the day. The sun was rising in all its splendid beauty; but the light only served to show the boy his own lonesomeness and desolation, as he sat, with bleeding feet and covered with dust, upon a door-step… He had no heart to beg, and there he sat.

He had been crouching on the step for some time, gazing listlessly at the coaches as they passed through, and thinking how strange it seemed that they could do with ease in a few hours what it had taken him a whole week of courage and determination beyond his years to accomplish, when he was roused by observing that a boy, who had passed him carelessly some minutes before, had returned, and was now surveying him most earnestly from the opposite side of the way. He took little heed of this at first; but the boy remained in the same attitude of close observation so long, that Oliver raised his head, and returned his steady look. Upon this, the boy crossed over, and, walking close up to Oliver, said,

'Hullo, my covey! What's the row?'

The boy who addressed this inquiry to the young wayfarer was about his own age, but one of the queerest-looking boys that Oliver had ever seen. He was a snub-nosed, flat-browed, common-faced boy enough; and as dirty a juvenile as one would wish to see; but he had got about him all the airs and manners of a man. He was short of his age, with rather bow-legs, and little sharp ugly eyes. His hat was stuck on the top of his head so slightly that it threatened to fall off every moment, and would have done so very often if the wearer had not had a knack of every now and then giving his head a sudden twitch, which brought it back to its old place again. He wore a man's coat, which reached nearly to his heels. He had turned the cuffs back halfway up his arm to get his hands out of the sleeves: apparently with the ultimate view of thrusting them into the pockets of his corduroy trousers, for there he kept them. He was, altogether, as roystering and swaggering a young gentleman as ever stood four feet six, or something less, in his bluchers.

'Hullo, my covey! What's the row?' said this strange young gentleman to Oliver.

'I am very hungry and tired,' replied Oliver: the tears standing in his eyes as he spoke. 'I have walked a long way. I have been walking these seven days.'

'Walking for sivin days!' said the young gentleman. 'Oh, I see. Beak's order, eh? But,' he added, noticing Oliver's look of surprise, 'I suppose you don't know what a beak is, my flash com-pan-i-on.'

Oliver mildly replied, that he had always heard a bird's mouth described by the term in question.

'My eyes, how green!' exclaimed the young gentleman. 'Why, a beak's a madg'strate; and when you walk by a beak's order, it's not straight forerd, but always a-going up, and niveir a-coming down agin... But come,' said the young gentleman; 'you want grub, and you shall have it. I'm at low-water-mark myself – only one bob and a magpie; but, *as* far *as* it goes, I'll fork out and stump. Up with you on your pins. There! Now then! Morrice!'

Assisting Oliver to rise, the young gentleman took him to an adjacent chandler's shop, where he purchased a sufficiency of ready-dressed ham and a half-quartern loaf, or, as he himself expressed it, 'a fourpenny bran'; the ham being kept clean and preserved from dust, by the ingenious expedient of making a hole in the loaf by pulling out a portion of the crumb, and stuffing it therein. Taking the bread under his arm, the young gentleman turned in to a small public-house, and led the way to a tap-room in the rear of the premises. Here, a pot of beer was brought in, by direction of the mysterious youth; and Oliver, falling to, at his new friend's bidding, made a long and hearty meal, during the progress of which, the strange boy eyed him from time to time with great attention.

'Going to London?' said the strange boy, when Oliver had at length concluded.

Charles Dickens, *Oliver Twist* (1837–8)

The City

Not long ago, about the closing in of an evening in autumn, I sat at the large bow window of the D– Coffee House in London. For some months I had been ill in health, but was now convalescent, and, with returning strength, found myself in one of those happy moods which are so precisely the converse of ennui... Merely to breathe was enjoyment, and I derived positive pleasure even from many of the legitimate sources of pain. I felt a calm but inquisitive interest in every thing. With a cigar in my mouth and a newspaper in my lap, I had been amusing myself for the greater part of the afternoon, now in poring over advertisements, now in observing the promiscuous company in the room, and now in peering through the smoky panes into the street.

This latter is one of the principal thoroughfares of the city, and had been very much crowded during the whole day. But, as the darkness came on, the throng momently increased; and, by the time the lamps were well lighted, two dense and continuous tides of population were rushing past the door.

With my brow to the glass, I was thus occupied in scrutinizing the mob, when suddenly there came into view a countenance (that of a decrepit old man, some sixty-five or seventy years of age) – a countenance which at once arrested and absorbed my whole attention, on account of the absolute idiosyncrasy of its expression. Any thing even remotely resembling that expression I had never seen before. I well remember that my first thought, upon beholding it, was that Retzch, had he viewed it, would have greatly preferred it to his own pictural incarnations of the fiend. As I endeavored, during the brief minute of my original survey, to form some analysis of the meaning conveyed, there arose confusedly and paradoxically within my mind, the ideas of vast mental power, of caution, of penuriousness, of avarice, of coolness, of malice, of blood thirstiness, of triumph, of merriment, of excessive terror, of intense – of supreme despair. I felt singularly aroused, startled, fascinated. 'How wild a history,' I said to myself, 'is written within that bosom!' Then came a craving desire to keep the man in view – to know more of him. Hurriedly putting on an overcoat, and seizing my hat and cane, I made my way into the street, and pushed through the crowd in the direction which I had seen him take; for he had already disappeared. With some little difficulty I at length came within sight of him, approached, and followed him closely, yet cautiously, so as not to attract his attention.

I had now a good opportunity of examining his person. He was short in stature, very thin, and apparently very feeble. His clothes, generally, were filthy and ragged; but as he came, now and then, within the strong glare of a lamp, I perceived that his linen, although dirty, was of beautiful texture; and my vision deceived me, or, through a rent in a closely-buttoned and evidently second-handed *roquelaire* which enveloped him, I caught a glimpse both of a diamond and of a dagger. These observations heightened my curiosity, and I resolved to follow the stranger whithersoever he should go.

It was now fully night-fall, and a thick humid fog hung over the city, soon ending in a settled and heavy rain. This change of weather had an odd effect upon the crowd, the whole of which was at once put into new commotion, and overshadowed by a world of umbrellas. The waver, the jostle, and the hum increased in a tenfold degree. For my own part I did not much regard the rain – the lurking of an old fever in my system rendering the moisture somewhat too dangerously pleasant. Tying a handkerchief about my mouth, I kept on. For half an hour the old man held his way with difficulty along the great thoroughfare; and I here walked close at his elbow through fear of losing sight of him. Never once turning his head to look back, he did not observe me. By and by he passed into a cross street, which, although densely filled with people, was not quite so much thronged as the main one he had quitted. Here a change in his demeanor became evident. He walked more slowly and with less object than before – more hesitatingly. He crossed and re-crossed the way repeatedly without apparent aim; and the press was still so thick that, at every such movement, I was obliged to follow him closely. The street was a narrow and long one, and his course lay within it for nearly an hour, during which the passengers had gradually diminished to about that number which is ordinarily seen at noon in Broadway near the Park – so vast a difference is there between a London populace and that of the most frequented American city. A second turn brought us into a square, brilliantly lighted, and overflowing with life. The old manner of the stranger reappeared. His chin fell upon his breast, while his eyes rolled wildly from under his knit brows, in every direction, upon those who hemmed him in. He urged his way steadily and perseveringly. I was surprised, however, to find, upon his having made the circuit of the square, that he turned and retraced his steps. Still more was I astonished to see him repeat the same walk several times – once nearly detecting me as he came round with a sudden movement.

In this exercise he spent another hour, at the end of which we met with far less interruption from passengers than at first. The rain fell fast; the air grew cool; and the people were retiring to their homes. With a gesture of impatience, the wanderer passed into a by-street comparatively deserted. Down this, some quarter of a mile long, he rushed with an activity I could not have dreamed of seeing in one so aged, and which put me to much trouble in pursuit. A few minutes brought us to a large and busy bazaar, with the localities of which the stranger appeared well acquainted, and where his original demeanor again became apparent, as he forced his way to and fro, without aim, among the host of buyers and sellers.

During the hour and a half, or thereabouts, which we passed in this place, it required much caution on my part to keep him within reach without attracting his observation. Luckily I wore a pair of caoutchouc over-shoes, and could move about in perfect silence. At no moment did he see that I watched him. He entered shop after shop, priced nothing, spoke no word, and looked at all objects with a wild and vacant stare. I was now utterly amazed at his behavior, and firmly resolved that we should not part until I had satisfied myself in some measure respecting him.

A loud-toned clock struck eleven, and the company were fast deserting the bazaar. A shop-keeper, in putting up a shutter, jostled the old man, and at the instant I saw a strong shudder come over his frame. He hurried into the street, looked anxiously around him for an instant, and then ran with incredible swiftness through many crooked and people-less lanes, until we emerged once more upon the great thoroughfare whence we had started – the street of the D– Hotel. It no longer wore, however, the same aspect. It was still brilliant with gas; but the rain fell fiercely, and there were few persons to be seen. The stranger grew pale. He walked moodily some paces up the once populous avenue, then, with a heavy sigh, turned in the direction of the river, and, plunging through a great variety of devious ways, came out, at length, in view of one of the principal theaters. It was about being closed, and the audience were thronging from the doors. I saw the old man gasp as if for breath while he threw himself amid the crowd; but I thought that the intense agony of his countenance had, in some measure, abated. His head again fell upon his breast; he appeared as I had seen him at first. I observed that he now took the course in which had gone the greater number of the audience – but, upon the whole, I was at a loss to comprehend the waywardness of his actions.

As he proceeded, the company grew more scattered, and his old uneasiness and vacillation were resumed. For some time he followed closely a party of some ten or twelve roisterers; but from this number one by one dropped off, until three only remained together, in a narrow and gloomy lane little frequented. The stranger paused, and, for a moment, seemed lost in thought; then, with every mark of agitation, pursued rapidly a route which brought us to the verge of the city, amid regions very different from those we had hitherto traversed. It was the most noisome quarter of London, where every thing wore the worst impress of the most deplorable poverty, and of the most desperate crime. By the dim light of an accidental lamp, tall, antique, worm-eaten, wooden tenements were seen tottering to their fall, in directions so many and capricious that scarce the semblance of a passage was discernible between them. The paving-stones lay at random, displaced from their beds by the rankly growing grass. Horrible filth festered in the dammed-up gutters. The whole atmosphere teemed with desolation. Yet, as we proceeded, the sounds of human life revived by sure degrees, and at length large bands of the most abandoned of a London populace were seen reeling to and fro. The spirits of the old man again flickered up, as a lamp which is near its death hour. Once more he strode onward with elastic tread. Suddenly a corner was turned, a blaze of light burst upon our sight, and we stood before one of the huge suburban temples of Intemperance – one of the palaces of the fiend, Gin.

It was now nearly daybreak, but a number of wretched inebriates still pressed in and out of the flaunting entrance. With a half shriek of joy the old man forced a passage within, resumed at once his original bearing, and stalked backward and forward, without apparent object, among the throng. He had not been thus long occupied, however, before a rush to the doors gave token that the host was closing them for the night. It was something even more intense than despair that I then observed upon the countenance of the singular being whom I had watched so pertinaciously. Yet he did not hesitate in his career, but, with a mad energy, retraced his steps at once, to the heart of the mighty London. Long and swiftly he fled, while I followed him in the wildest amazement, resolute not to abandon a scrutiny in which I now felt an interest all-absorbing. The sun arose while we proceeded, and, when we had once again reached that most thronged mart of the populous town, the street of the D– Hotel, it presented an appearance of human bustle and activity scarcely inferior to what I had seen on the evening before. And here, long, amid the momently increasing confusion, did I persist in my pursuit of the stranger. But, as usual, he walked to and fro, and during the day did not pass from out the turmoil of that street. And, as the shades of the second evening came on, I grew wearied unto death, and, stopping fully in front of the wanderer, gazed at him steadfastly in the face. He noticed me not, but resumed his solemn walk, while I, ceasing to follow, remained absorbed in contemplation. 'This old man,' I said at length, 'is the type and the genius of deep crime. He refuses to be alone. *He is the man of the crowd.* It will be in vain to follow, for I shall learn no more of him, nor of his deeds...'

Edgar Allan Poe, 'The Man of The Crowd' (1840)

Close to Things

Regaining the river they walked on in the direction of Notre Dame, delayed now and again by the young man's irresistible tendency to linger over the bookstalls, and by his ever-fresh response to the shifting beauties of the scene. For two years his eyes had been subdued to the atmospheric effects of London, to the mysterious fusion of darkly piled city and low-lying bituminous sky; and the transparency of the French air, which left the green gardens and silvery stones so classically clear yet so softly harmonized, struck him as having a kind of conscious intelligence. Every line of the architecture, every arch of the bridges, the very sweep of the strong bright river between them, while contributing to this effect, sent forth each a separate appeal to some sensitive memory; so that, for Darrow, a walk through the Paris streets was always like the unrolling of a vast tapestry from which countless stored fragrances were shaken out.

Edith Wharton, *The Reef* (1912)

It's Quicker on Foot

And now Joseph putting his head out of the coach, cried out, 'Never believe me if yonder be not our Parson Adams walking along with out his horse!'

'On my word, and so he is,' says Slipslop, 'and as sure as twopence he hath left him behind at the inn.'

Indeed, true it is, the Parson had exhibited a fresh instance of his absence of mind, for he was so pleased with having got Joseph into the coach, that he never once thought of the beast in the stable; and, finding his legs as nimble as he desired, he sallied out, brandishing a crab-stick, and had kept on before the coach, mending and slackening his pace occasionally, so that he had never been much more or less than a quarter of a mile distant from it.

Mrs Slipslop desired the coachman to overtake him, which he attempted, but in vain: for the faster he drove, the faster ran the Parson, often crying out, 'Aye, Aye, catch me if you can,' till at length the coachman swore he would as soon attempt to drive after a greyhound, and, giving the Parson two or three hearty curses, he cried, 'Softly, softly boys,' to his horses, which the civil beasts immediately obeyed.

But we will be more courteous to our Reader than he was to Mrs Slipslop, and leaving the coach and its company to pursue their journey, we will carry our reader on after Parson Adams, who stretched forwards without once looking behind him, till, having left the coach full three miles in his rear, he came to a place where, by keeping the extremest track to the right, it was just barely possible for a human creature to miss his way. This track, however, did he keep, as indeed he had a wonderful capacity at these kinds of bare possibilities, and, travelling about three miles over the plain, he arrived at the summit of a hill, whence looking a great way backwards, and perceiving no coach in sight, he sat himself down on the turf, and pulling out his Aeschylus, determined to wait here for its arrival.

Henry Fielding, *Joseph Andrews* (1742)

Curing her Restlessness

She felt the need of rapid movement. She must walk out in spite of the rain. Happily, there was a thin place in the curtain of clouds which seemed to promise that now, about noon, the day had a mind to clear up. Caterina thought to herself, 'I will walk to the Mosslands, and carry Mr Bates the comforter I have made for him, and then Lady Cheverel will not wonder so much about my going out.' At the hall door she found Rupert, the old bloodhound, stationed on the mat, with the determination that the first person who was sensible enough to take a walk that morning should have the honour of his approbation and society. As he thrust his great black and tawny head under her hand, and wagged his tail with vigorous eloquence, and reached the climax of his welcome by jumping up to lick her face, which was at a convenient licking height for him, Caterina felt quite grateful to the old dog for his friendliness. Animals are such agreeable friends – they ask no questions, they pass no criticisms.

The 'Mosslands' was a remote part of the grounds, encircled by the little stream issuing from the pool, and certainly, for a wet day, Caterina could hardly have chosen a less suitable walk, for though the rain was abating, and presently ceased altogether, there was still a smart shower falling from the trees that arched over the greater part of her way. But she found the desired relief from her feverish excitement in labouring along the wet paths with an umbrella that made her arm ache. This amount of exertion was to her tiny body what a day's hunting often was to Mr Gilfil, who at times had *his* fits of jealousy and sadness to get rid of, and wisely had recourse to nature's innocent opium – fatigue.

George Eliot, *Scenes of Clerical Life* (1858)

Curing his Restlessness

When it seems we have finally decided to stay home of an evening, have slipped into our smoking jackets, are sitting at a lit table after supper, and have taken out some piece of work or game at the conclusion of which we customarily go to bed, when the weather outside is inclement, which makes it perfectly understandable that we are staying at home, when we have been sitting quietly at our table for so long that our going out would provoke great astonishment, when the stairwell is dark and the front gate is bolted, and when, in spite of all, in a sudden access of restlessness, we get up, change into a jacket, and straightaway look ready to go out, explain that we are compelled to go out, and after a brief round of goodbyes actually do so, leaving behind a greater or lesser amount of irritation depending on the noise we make closing the front door behind us, when we find ourselves down on the street, with limbs that respond to the unexpected freedom they have come into with a particular suppleness, when by this one decision we feel all the decisiveness in us mobilised, when we recognize with uncommon clarity that we have more energy than we need to accomplish and to withstand the most abrupt changes, and when in this mood we walk down the longest streets – then for the duration of that evening we have escaped our family once and for all, so it drifts into vaporousness, whereas we ourselves, as indisputable and sharp and black as a silhouette, smacking the backs of our thighs, come into our true nature.

And all this may even be accentuated if, at this late hour, we go to seek out some friend, to see how he is doing.

Franz Kafka, *The Sudden Walk* (1913)
Translated by Michael Hoffman

Strolling Stirs the Creative Juices

Four hours gave me ample time to carry out my plan, since on this occasion I merely wanted to perform a simple excursion around my room. If the first journey lasted forty-two days, this was because I had not been in any position to ensure that it took a shorter time. Nor did I wish to be constrained to travelling much in a coach, as before, since I am convinced that a traveller on foot sees many things that escape a man who travels with the post. So I decided to go on foot and on horseback alternately, depending on the circumstances: a new method which I have not yet revealed, and whose usefulness will soon be apparent. Finally, I resolved to take notes en route, and to write down my observations as and when I made them, so as not to forget anything.

In order to put my enterprise in shape, and give it an increased chance of success, I reflected that it would be good to begin by composing a dedicatory epistle, and writing it in verse to make it more interesting. But two difficulties caused me some perplexity and almost made me give up, despite all the benefits I could derive from the project. The first was knowing to whom I should address the epistle, the second, how on earth I should go about writing verse. Then I remembered, appropriately enough, having read somewhere that the celebrated Pope never composed anything of interest without being obliged to declaim loud and long, and to walk energetically round and round his room so to stir up his creative juices. Thereupon, I tried to imitate him. I took the poetry of Ossian and recited it aloud, striding up and down so as to raise myself to a pitch of enthusiasm.

And I soon saw this method did indeed imperceptibly exalt my imagination, and gave me a secret sense of my poetic capabilities which I would certainly have turned to good advantage, going on to compose my dedicatory verse epistle with great success, if I had not unfortunately forgotten the fact that the ceiling of my room sloped down; its sudden descent prevented my forehead from travelling forward the same distance as my feet in the direction I had taken. I banged my head against that wretched sloping ceiling so hard that the roof of the house was given quite a jolt: the sparrows who had been asleep under the tiles flew off in alarm, and the collision made me take three steps backward.

Whilst I was walking around in this way to stimulate my imagination, a pretty young woman who was living below me, surprised at the noise I was making, and thinking perhaps that I was throwing a ball in my room, made her husband come up and find out what had caused the noise. I was still quite stunned by the contusion I had suffered, when the door half opened. An elderly man, wearing a melancholy expression, stuck his head in, and allowed his gaze to wander around the room. When his surprise at finding me alone had faded, he finally said, in vexed tones, 'My wife has a migraine, Sir. Allow me to point out to you that...'

I immediately interrupted him, and my style reflected the sublimity of my thoughts.

'Worthy messenger of my lovely neighbour,' I told him in proper bardic style, 'why do your eyes gleam beneath your bushy eyebrows, like two meteors in the black forest of Cromba? Your beautiful partner is a ray of light, and I would die a thousand times over rather than deliberately disturb her repose; but your expression, O worthy messenger... your expression is as grim as the most remote recess in the cave of

Camora, when the great and lofty clouds of the tempest cover the face of the night, and weigh down on the silent countryside of Morven.'

My neighbour, who had apparently never read Ossian's poetry, unfortunately took the outburst of divine inspiration that had stimulated me for an attack of madness, and seemed really perplexed. Since I had no intention of offending him, I offered him a seat and asked him to sit down; but I realised he was slowly beating a retreat, making the sign of the cross over himself as he murmured, '*È matto, per Bacco, è matto!*' – 'He's mad, by Bacchus, he's mad!'

Xavier De Maistre,
A Nocturnal Expedition Around My Room (1825)
Translated by Andrew Brown

A Word about Feet

The footsteps outside at any given moment were such as one might hear in any hotel; and yet, taken as a whole, there was something very strange about them...

First, there came a long rush of rapid little steps, such as a light man might make in winning a walking race. At a certain point they stopped and changed to a sort of slow, swinging stamp, numbering not a quarter of the steps, but occupying about the same time. The moment the last echoing step had died away would come again the run or ripple of light, hurrying feet, and then again the thud of the heavier walking. It was certainly the same pair of boots, partly because (as has been said) there were no other boots about, and partly because they had a small but unmistakable creak in them. Father Brown had the kind of head that cannot help asking questions; and on this apparently trivial question his head almost split. He had seen men run in order to jump. He had seen men run in order to slide. But why on earth should a man run in order to walk? Or, again, why should he walk in order to run? Yet no other description would cover the antics of this invisible pair of legs. The man was either walking very fast down one side of the corridor in order to walk very slowly down the other half; or he was walking very slow at one end to have the rapture of walking fast at the other...

Father Brown began to ask himself with more exactness what the steps suggested. Taking the slow step first; it certainly was not the step of the proprietor. Men of his type walk with a rapid waddle, or they sit still. It could not be any servant or messenger waiting for directions. It did not sound like it. The poorer orders (in an oligarchy) sometimes lurch about when they are slightly drunk, but generally, and especially in such gorgeous scenes, they stand or sit in constrained attitudes. No; that heavy yet springy step, with a kind of careless emphasis, belongs to only one of the animals of this earth. It was a gentleman of western Europe, and probably one who has never worked for his living.

G.K. Chesterton, *The Innocence of Father Brown* (1911)

Legs

Mrs Mountstuart touched a thrilling chord. 'In spite of men's hateful modern costume, you see he has a leg.'

That is, the leg of the born cavalier is before you: and obscure it as you will, dress degenerately, there it is for ladies who have eyes. You see it: or you see *he* has it. Miss Isabel and Miss Eleanor disputed the incidence of the emphasis, but surely, though a slight difference of meaning may be heard, either will do: many, with a good show of reason, throw the accent upon *leg*. And the ladies knew for a fact that Willoughby's leg was exquisite; he had a cavalier court-suit in his wardrobe. Mrs Mountstuart signified that the leg was to be seen because it was a burning leg. There it is, and it will shine through! He has the leg of Rochester, Buckingham, Dorset, Suckling; the leg that smiles, winks, is obsequious to you, yet perforce of beauty self-satisfied; that twinkles to a tender midway between imperiousness and seductiveness, audacity and discretion; between 'You shall worship me,' and 'I am devoted to you'; is your lord, your slave, alternately and in one. It is a leg of ebb and flow and high-tide ripples. Such a leg, when it is done with pretending to retire, will walk straight into the hearts of women.

George Meredith, *The Egoist* (1879)

Equipment

Enter Landlord with first and second pedestrian, dressed in sailor's jackets and trousers, knapsacks at their backs, umbrellas etc.

LANDLORD	Two gentlemen on foot, Sir. Your room will be ready immediately. [*Exit*]
BOB	Foot! Poor Devils.
1st PED	We do not interrupt you, I hope, Sir?
BOB	No. What you've walked have you? Why do you walk as sailors?
1st PED	The dress is light, and well adapted for walking.
BOB	But a'n't you afraid of being taken up?
2nd PED	No Sir. We injure no one, why should anyone injure us?
BOB	You must be a little tired and foot-sore, I think?
1st PED	Neither, Sir; we are used to it, and suffer no inconvenience whatsoever.
BOB	Used to it! What, you've come some way?
2nd PED	Some hundreds of miles, Sir.
BOB	What, going home? or going to see some friends?

| 2nd PED | Neither, Sir. Travelling for pleasure. |
| BOB | That's a good one. Travelling on foot for pleasure! |

James Plumptre, *The Lakers* (1798)

The Passeggiatta: 'Fifty people have noticed her'

'Gracious me!' Daisy exclaimed, 'I don't want to do anything improper. There's an easy way to settle it.' She continued to glance at Winterbourne. 'The Pincio is only a hundred yards distant; and if Mr Winterbourne were as polite as he pretends, he would offer to walk with me!'

Winterbourne's politeness hastened to affirm itself, and the young girl gave him gracious leave to accompany her. They passed downstairs before her mother, and at the door Winterbourne perceived Mrs Miller's carriage drawn up, with the ornamental courier whose acquaintance he had made at Vevey seated within.

'Goodbye, Eugenio!' cried Daisy; 'I'm going to take a walk.'

The distance from the Via Gregoriana to the beautiful garden at the other end of the Pincian Hill is, in fact, rapidly traversed. As the day was splendid, however, and the concourse of vehicles, walkers, and loungers numerous, the young Americans found their progress much delayed. This fact was highly agreeable to Winterbourne, in spite of his consciousness of his singular situation. The slow-moving, idly gazing Roman crowd bestowed much attention upon the extremely pretty young foreign lady who was passing through it upon his arm; and he wondered what on earth had been in Daisy's mind when she proposed to expose herself, unattended, to its appreciation. His own mission, to her sense, apparently, was to consign her to the hands of Mr Giovanelli; but Winterbourne, at once annoyed and gratified, resolved that he would do no such thing...

When they had passed the gate of the Pincian Gardens, Miss Miller began to wonder where Mr Giovanelli might be. 'We had better go straight to that place in front,' she said, 'where you look at the view.'

'I certainly shall not help you to find him,' Winterbourne declared.

'Then I shall find him without you,' cried Miss Daisy.

'You certainly won't leave me!' cried Winterbourne.

She burst into her little laugh. 'Are you afraid you'll get lost – or run over? But there's Giovanelli, leaning against that tree. He's staring at the women in the carriages: did you ever see anything so cool?'

Winterbourne perceived at some distance a little man standing with folded arms, nursing his cane. He had a handsome face, an artfully poised hat, a glass in one eye, and a nosegay in his buttonhole. Winterbourne looked at him a moment and then said, 'Do you mean to speak to that man?'

'Do I mean to speak to him? Why, you don't suppose I mean to communicate by signs?'...

The gentleman with the nosegay in his bosom had now perceived our two friends, and was approaching the young girl with obsequious rapidity. He bowed to Winterbourne as well as to the latter's companion; he had a brilliant smile, an intelligent eye; Winterbourne thought him not a bad-looking fellow. But he nevertheless said to Daisy, 'No, he's not the right one.'

Daisy evidently had a natural talent for performing introductions; she mentioned the name of each of her companions to the other. She strolled alone with one of them on each side of her; Mr Giovanelli, who spoke English very cleverly – Winterbourne afterwards learned that he had practised the idiom upon a great many American heiresses – addressed her a great deal of very polite nonsense; he was extremely urbane, and the young American, who said nothing, reflected upon that profundity of Italian cleverness that enables people to appear more gracious in proportion as they are more acutely disappointed. Giovanelli, of course, had counted upon something more intimate; he had not bargained for a party of three. But he kept his temper in a manner that suggested far-stretching intentions. Winterbourne flattered himself that he had taken his measure. 'He is not a gentleman,' said the young American; 'he is only a clever imitation of one. He is a music master, or a penny-a-liner, or a third-rate artist. Damn his good looks!' Mr Giovanelli had certainly a very pretty face; but Winterbourne felt a superior indignation at his own lovely fellow countrywoman's not knowing the difference between a spurious gentleman and a real one...

She had been walking some quarter of an hour, attended by her two cavaliers, and responding in a tone of very childish gaiety, as it seemed to Winterbourne, to the pretty speeches of Mr Giovanelli, when a carriage that had detached itself from the revolving train drew up beside the path. At the same moment Winterbourne perceived that his friend Mrs Walker – the lady whose house he had lately left – was seated in the vehicle and was beckoning to him. Leaving Miss Miller's side, he hastened to obey her summons. Mrs Walker was flushed; she wore an excited air.

'It is really too dreadful,' she said. 'That girl must not do this sort of thing. She must not walk here with you two men. Fifty people have noticed her.'

Winterbourne raised his eyebrows. 'I think it's a pity to make too much fuss about it.'

'It's a pity to let the girl ruin herself!'

'She is very innocent,' said Winterbourne.

'She's very crazy!' cried Mrs Walker. 'Did you ever see anything so imbecile as her mother? After you had all left me just now, I could not sit still for thinking of it. It seemed too pitiful, not even to attempt to save her. I ordered the carriage and put on my bonnet, and came here as quickly as possible. Thank Heaven I have found you!'...

'Get in here, sir,' she said to Winterbourne, indicating the place beside her. The young man answered that he felt bound to accompany Miss Miller, whereupon Mrs Walker declared that if he refused her this favour she would never speak to him again. She was evidently in earnest. Winterbourne overtook Daisy and her companion, and, offering the young girl his hand, told her that Mrs Walker had made an imperious claim upon his society. He expected that in answer she would say something rather free, something to commit herself still further to that 'recklessness' from which Mrs Walker had so charitably endeavoured to dissuade her. But she only shook his hand, hardly looking at him, while Mr Giovanelli bade him farewell with a too emphatic flourish of the hat.

Winterbourne was not in the best possible humour as he took his seat in Mrs Walker's victoria. 'That was not clever of you,' he said candidly, while the vehicle mingled again with the throng of carriages...

The carriage was traversing that part of the Pincian Garden that overhangs the wall of Rome and overlooks the beautiful Villa Borghese. It is bordered by a large parapet, near which there are several seats. One of the seats, at a distance, was occupied by a gentleman and a lady, towards whom Mrs Walker gave a toss of her head. At the same moment these persons rose and walked toward the parapet. Winterbourne had asked the coachman to stop; he now descended from the carriage. His companion looked at him a moment in silence; then, while he raised his hat, she drove majestically away. Winterbourne stood there; he had turned his eyes toward Daisy and her cavalier. They evidently saw no one; they were too deeply occupied with each other. When they reached the low garden wall, they stood a moment looking off at the great flat-topped pine clusters of the Villa Borghese; then Giovanelli seated himself familiarly upon the broad ledge of the wall. The western sun in the opposite sky sent out a brilliant shaft through a couple of cloud bars, whereupon Daisy's companion took her parasol out of her hands and opened it. She came a little nearer, and he held the parasol over her; then, still holding it, he let it rest upon her shoulder, so that both of their heads were hidden from Winterbourne. This young man lingered a moment, then he began to walk. But he walked – not towards the couple with the parasol; towards the residence of his aunt, Mrs Costello.

Henry James, *Daisy Miller* (1879)

The Passeggiatta: 'Show off his legs'

Every evening above five, he appeared on the Cours Boieldieu on his way to drink a glass of absinthe at the Café de la Comédie, though before entering this establishment he made a point of taking a turn along the promenade to show off his legs, his waist, his moustache.

The town's men of business, who also walked there with their hands behind their backs and their minds full of their business, talking of markets rising and falling, nevertheless gave a glance in his direction and murmured, 'By Jove! Now there's a fine figure of a man!' And they knew who he was, 'Look it's Captain Epivent. Say what you like, he's a hell of a fellow.'

When women passed him, they gave a slight movement of the head which was very droll, a sort of maidenly quiver, as though they had come over all weak or felt undressed before him. They lowered their eyes with just the shadow of a smile on their lips, wishing to be thought charming and to receive a glance from him. When he walked with a comrade, the comrade never failed to mutter enviously every time he witnessed the usual goings on, 'Old Epivent's got the luck of the devil!'

Among the town's whores there was a struggle, a race, to see who would get him first. They all turned up at the Cours Boieldieu at five, the officers' regular time, and in twos they trailed their skirts from one end of the promenade to the other while lieutenants, captains, and commanders, also in twos, trailed their sabres over the pavement before entering the café.

One evening, the beautiful Irma – who was rumoured to be the mistress of Monsieur Templier-Papon, a rich manufacturer – ordered her driver to halt opposite the Café de la Comédie. As she stepped down, she gave every impression that she was about to buy some writing paper or order some visiting cards from Monsieur Paulard, the engraver, though the whole thing was of course engineered to allow her to pass in front of the officers' table and to give Captain Epivent a look signifying: 'Ready when you are,' which was so transparent that Colonel Prune who was drinking a glass of absinthe with his Lieutenant-Colonel was unable to prevent himself muttering, 'The swine's got the luck of the devil!'

What the Colonel said was repeated; and the next day Captain Epivent, in full dress uniform, delighted at having such high level approval, strolled by (and did so again several times) under the windows of the beautiful Irma.

She saw him. She appeared at her window. She smiled.

The same evening he became her lover.

Guy de Maupassant, 'Bed 29' (1902)
Translated by David Coward

On an Even Footing with Him

And suddenly... and suddenly I took revenge in the most simple, in the most ingenious way! The brightest of ideas suddenly dawned on me. Sometimes on holidays I would go down to Nevsky Avenue after three o'clock and enjoy a stroll along the sunny side. That is, I didn't enjoy a stroll there at all, but experienced countless tortures, humiliations and bilious attacks, but that was probably what I needed. Like a loach, I darted up and down between passers-by in the most unattractive manner, giving way incessantly, now to generals, now to officers of the Horse Guards and Hussars, now to fine ladies; at these moments I felt convulsive pains in the heart and a burning in the spine at the mere idea of the wretchedness and vulgarity of my little darting figure. It was excruciating torment, incessant, unbearable humiliation at the thought, which turned into an incessant and direct sense, that I was a fly before all this society, a vile, obscene fly – more intelligent than all, more developed than all, more noble than all, that goes without saying – but a fly, incessantly giving way to all, humiliated by all, and insulted by all. Why did I inflict this torture upon myself, why did I go to Nevsky? I don't know, but I was simply *drawn* there at every opportunity.

… after the incident with the officer I began to be drawn there even more powerfully: it was on Nevsky that I met him most, it was there that I feasted my eyes on him. He too went there most on holidays. Although he would also turn out of the way before generals and persons of high rank, and also swung to and fro between them like a loach, still the likes of me, or even those rather smarter than the likes of me, he simply crushed; he walked straight at them, as though before him was an empty space, and in no instance whatsoever did he give way. I reveled in my malice, watching him, and… every time I turned aside before him in embitterment. It tortured me that even in the street I couldn't possibly be on an equal footing with him. 'Why are you sure to turn aside first?' I badgered myself in furious hysteria, waking up sometimes after two in the morning. 'Why specifically you and not him? There's no law about it, is there, it's not written down anywhere, is it? Well, so let it be divided equally, as is usually the case when tactful people meet; half the time he'll give way, and half the time you, and you'll both pass by, mutually respecting one another.' But that's not how it was, and it was I that turned aside all the same, while he didn't even notice I was giving way to him. And then the most amazing idea suddenly dawned on me. 'And what,' I dreamed up, 'what if I were to meet with him and… not step aside? Deliberately not step aside, even if it meant I had to push him: how would that be, eh?' This daring idea so took hold of me little by little that it gave me no peace. I dreamt about it incessantly, dreadfully, and I deliberately went to Nevsky more often to picture to myself still more clearly how I would do it, when I would do it. I was in raptures. More and more this intention seemed to me both probable and possible. 'It stands to reason, not exactly push,' I thought, in my joy already mellowing in advance, 'but you know, simply not step aside, bump up against him, not so it hurts a lot, but you know, shoulder to shoulder, just exactly as much as he bumps me, I bump him too just as much.' I finally made up my mind completely. But preparations took a very great deal of time. The first thing was that, when carrying it out, I needed to be in a more highly respectable state, and to do something about my suit. 'Just in case, if, for example, a public incident starts (and the public there is something extraordinary: the Countess is there, Prince D.'s there, the whole of literature's there, out walking, I must be well dressed; that makes an impression, and in a certain way will put us right on an equal footing in the eyes of high society.' With this aim I asked for my salary in advance and bought black gloves and a respectable hat at Churkin's. The black gloves seemed to me both more dignified and more *bon ton* than the lemon ones I had designs on at first. 'The colour's too harsh, it's too much as if a man wants to show off,' and I didn't take the lemon ones. A good shirt with white ivory cufflinks I had already prepared long before, but my greatcoat delayed me greatly. In itself, my greatcoat wasn't at all bad, it was warm, but it was wadded, and the collar was of raccoon, which really was the height of plebeianism. The collar needed to be changed at all costs and a beaver one acquired, like officers have. To do this I started going around Gostiny Dvor, and after several attempts I aimed for a cheap German beaver collar. These German beaver collars, although they do wear out very quickly and take on the most wretched appearance, at first, when they're new, look really very respectable even, and after all, I did only need it for the one occasion. I asked the price: it was expensive, though.

Upon thorough consideration I made up my mind to sell my raccoon collar, while the sum that was lacking, and which was for me a very significant one, I made up my mind to ask to borrow from Anton Antonych Setochkin, my Head of Section, a humble man, but a serious and positive one, who lent money to no one, but to whom I had once, when taking up my position, been especially recommended by the significant figure who had appointed me to the post. I went through dreadful torment. Asking Anton Antonych for money seemed to me monstrous and shameful. For two or three nights I couldn't even sleep, and generally I got little sleep at that time, I was in a fever; all muddled up, my heart would somehow stop beating or suddenly start leaping, leaping, leaping!... At first Anton Antonovich was surprised, then he frowned, then he considered things and gave me the loan after all, taking from me a signed statement of his right to have back the money given on loan from my salary in two weeks' time. Thus everything was at last ready; the handsome beaver reigned in the filthy raccoon's place, and I gradually began getting down to business. It just wasn't possible to resolve upon action all at once, any old how; this business needed to be arranged skilfully; gradually was just the way. But I confess that after numerous attempts I was even on the point of beginning to despair: no way do we bump into one another – and that's all there is to it! Do I not prepare myself, do I not intend to do it – at any moment now, it seems, we'll bump into one another, but what do I see – again I've given way, and he's passed by without even noticing me. I even said prayers as I approached him for God to inspire me with decisiveness. On one occasion I was even on the point of actually resolving upon it completely, but it ended with my just getting under his feet, because at the very last instant, at a distance of some three inches, I didn't have the courage. Perfectly calmly, he passed over me, and I, like a little ball, flew off to one side. That night I was ill again, in a fever and raving. And suddenly everything ended in the best possible way. The night before, I decided definitively not to carry out my ruinous intention and to abandon this entire business undone, and with that aim I went out onto Nevsky for the last time, just to look and see how I could leave it all undone. Suddenly, three paces away from my enemy, I unexpectedly made up my mind, screwed up my eyes, and we bumped one another solidly, shoulder to shoulder! I didn't give an inch, and passed by on an absolutely even footing! He didn't even look round, and pretended he hadn't noticed, but he only pretended, I'm certain of it. I'm certain of it to this day! It stands to reason, I came off worse; he was stronger, but that wasn't the point. The point was that I'd achieved my aim, stood up for my dignity, hadn't conceded a single step and had publicly put myself on an equal social footing with him. I returned home completely avenged for everything. I was in raptures. I was triumphant and singing Italian arias.

Fyodor Dostoevsky, *Notes from the Underground* (1864)
Translated by Hugh Aplin

Summat about Streetwalkers

They quitted the glare of the gas-lighted room, and came out into the street. Unceasing, soaking rain was falling. The very lamps seemed obscured by the damp upon the glass, and their light reached but to a little distance from the posts. The streets were cleared of passers-by; not a creature seemed stirring, except here and there a drenched policeman in his oilskin cape. Barton wished the others good-night, and set off home. He had gone through a street or two, when he heard a step behind him; but he did not care to stop and see who it was. A little further, and the person quickened step, and touched his arm very lightly. He turned, and saw, even by the darkness visible of that badly lighted street, that the woman who stood by him was of no doubtful profession. It was told by her faded finery, all unfit to meet the pelting of that pitiless storm; the gauze bonnet, once pink, now dirty white; the muslin gown, all draggled, and soaking wet up to the very knees; the gay-coloured barège shawl, closely wrapped round the form, which yet shivered and shook, as the woman whispered, 'I want to speak to you.'

He swore an oath, and bade her begone.

'I really do. Don't send me away. I'm so out of breath, I cannot say what I would all at once.' She put her hand to her side, and caught her breath with evident pain.

'I tell thee I'm not the man for thee,' adding an opprobrious name. 'Stay,' said he, as a thought suggested by her voice flashed across him. He gripped her arm – the arm he had just before shaken off – and dragged her, faintly resisting, to the nearest lamp-post. He pushed the bonnet back, and roughly held the face she would fain have averted, to the light, and in her large, unnaturally bright grey eyes, her lovely mouth, half open, as if imploring the forbearance she could not ask for in words, he saw at once the long-lost Esther; she who had caused his wife's death. Much was like the gay creature of former years; but the glaring paint, the sharp features, the changed expression of the whole! But most of all, he loathed the dress; and yet the poor thing, out of her little choice of attire, had put on the plainest she had, to come on that night's errand.

'So it's thee, is it? It's thee!' exclaimed John, as he ground his teeth, and shook her with passion. 'I've looked for thee long at corners o' streets, and such like places. I knew I should find thee at last. Thee'll maybe bethink thee o' some words I spoke, which put thee up at th' time; summut about street-walkers; but oh no! thou art none o' them naughts; no one thinks thou art, who sees thy fine draggle-tailed dress, and thy pretty pink cheeks!' stopping for very want of breath.

'Oh, mercy! John, mercy! listen to me for Mary's sake!'

She meant his daughter, but the name only fell on his ear as belonging to his wife; and it was adding fuel to the fire. In vain did her face grow deadly pale around the vivid circle of paint, in vain did she gasp for mercy – he burst forth again.

'And thou names that name to me! and thou thinks the thought of her will bring thee mercy! Dost thou know it was thee who killed her, as sure as ever Cain killed Abel. She'd loved thee as her own, and she trusted thee as her own, and when thou wert gone she never held head up again, but died in less than a three week; and at her judgment day she'll rise, and point to thee as her murderer; or if she don't, I will.'

He flung her, trembling, sinking, fainting, from him, and strode away. She fell with a feeble scream against the lamp-post, and lay there in her weakness, unable to rise. A policeman came up in time to see the close of these occurrences, and concluding from Esther's unsteady, reeling fall, that she was tipsy, he took her in her half- unconscious state to the lock-ups for the night. The superintendent of that abode of vice and misery was roused from his dozing watch through the dark hours, by half-delirious wails and moanings, which he reported as arising from intoxication. If he had listened, he would have heard these words, repeated in various forms, but always in the same anxious, muttering way.

'He would not listen to me; what can I do? He would not listen to me, and I wanted to warn him! Oh, what shall I do to save Mary's child! What shall I do? How can I keep her from being such a one as I am; such a wretched, loathsome creature! She was listening just as I listened, and loving just as I loved, and the end will be just like my end. How shall I save her? She won't hearken to warning, or heed it more than I did: and who loves her well enough to watch over her as she should be watched? God keep her from harm! And yet I won't pray for her; sinner that I am! Can my prayers be heard? No! they'll only do harm. How shall I save her? He would not listen to me.'

So the night wore away. The next morning she was taken up to the New Bailey. It was a clear case of disorderly vagrancy, and she was committed to prison for a month. How much might happen in that time!

Elizabeth Gaskell, *Mary Barton* (1848)

Walking and Wooing: Progress

When all of the house that was open to general inspection had been seen, they returned downstairs and, taking leave of the housekeeper, were consigned over to the gardener, who met them at the hall-door.

As they walked across the lawn towards the river, Elizabeth turned back to look again; her uncle and aunt stopped also: and while the former was conjecturing as to the date of the building, the owner of it himself suddenly came forward from the road which led behind it to the stables.

They were within twenty yards of each other, and so abrupt was his appearance that it was impossible to avoid his sight. Their eyes instantly met, and the cheeks of each were overspread with the deepest blush. He absolutely started, and for a moment seemed immovable from surprise; but shortly recovering himself, advanced towards the party, and spoke to Elizabeth, if not in terms of perfect composure, at least of perfect civility.

She had instinctively turned away; but, stopping on his approach, received his compliments with an embarrassment impossible to be overcome. Had his first appearance, or his resemblance to the picture they had just been examining, been insufficient to assure the other two that they now saw Mr Darcy, the gardener's expression of surprise, on beholding his master, must immediately have told it. They stood a little aloof while he was talking to their niece, who, astonished and confused, scarcely dared lift her eyes to his face, and knew not what answer she returned to his civil enquiries after her family. Amazed at the alteration in his manner since they last parted, every sentence that he uttered was increasing her embarrassment; and every idea of the impropriety of her being found there recurring to her mind, the few minutes in which they continued together were some of the most uncomfortable of her life. Nor did he seem much more at ease: when he spoke, his accent had none of its usual sedateness; and he repeated his enquiries as to the time of her having left Longbourn, and of her stay in Derbyshire, so often, and in so hurried a way, as plainly spoke the distraction of his thoughts.

At length, every idea seemed to fail him; and, after standing a few moments without saying a word, he suddenly recollected himself, and took leave.

The others then joined her, and expressed their admiration of his figure; but Elizabeth heard not a word, and, wholly engrossed by her own feelings, followed them in silence. She was overpowered by shame and vexation. Her coming there was the most unfortunate, the most ill-judged thing in the world! How strange must it appear to him! In what a disgraceful light might it not strike so vain a man! It might seem as if she had purposely thrown herself in his way again! Oh! why did she come? or, why did he thus come a day before he was expected? Had they been only ten minutes sooner, they should have been beyond the reach of his discrimination; for it was plain that he was that moment arrived, that moment alighted from his horse or his carriage. She blushed again and again over the perverseness of the meeting. And his behaviour, so strikingly altered – what could it mean? That he should even speak to her was amazing! – but to speak with such civility, to inquire after her family!…

They had now entered a beautiful walk by the side of the water, and every step was bringing forward a nobler fall of ground, or a finer reach of the woods to which they were approaching; but it was some time before Elizabeth was sensible of any of it; and, though she answered mechanically to the repeated appeals of her uncle and aunt, and seemed to direct her eyes to such objects as they pointed out, she distinguished no part of the scene. Her thoughts were all fixed on that one spot of Pemberley House, whichever it might be, where Mr Darcy then was. She longed to know what at that moment was passing in his mind – in what manner he thought of her, and whether, in defiance of everything, she was still dear to him. Perhaps he had been civil only because he felt himself at ease; yet there had been *that* in his voice, which was not like ease. Whether he had felt more of pain or of pleasure in seeing her she could not tell, but he certainly had not seen her with composure.

At length, however, the remarks of her companions on her absence of mind roused her, and she felt the necessity of appearing more like herself.

They entered the woods, and bidding adieu to the river for a while, ascended some of the higher grounds; whence, in spots where the opening of the trees gave the eye power to wander, were many charming views of the valley, the opposite hills, with the long range of woods overspreading many, and occasionally part of the stream. Mr Gardiner expressed a wish of going round the whole park, but feared it might be beyond a walk. With a triumphant smile, they were told that it was ten miles round. It settled the matter; and they pursued the accustomed circuit; which brought them again, after some time, in a descent among hanging woods, to the edge of the water, in one of its narrowest parts. They crossed it by a simple bridge, in character with the general air of the scene: it was a spot less adorned than any they had yet visited; and the valley, here contracted into a glen, allowed room only for the stream and a narrow walk amidst the rough coppice-wood that bordered it. Elizabeth longed to explore its windings; but when they had crossed the bridge, and perceived their distance from the house, Mrs Gardiner, who was not a great walker, could go no farther, and thought only of returning to the carriage as quickly as possible. Her niece was, therefore, obliged to submit, and they took their way towards the house on the opposite side of the river, in the nearest direction; but their progress was slow, for Mr Gardiner, though seldom able to indulge the taste, was very fond of fishing, and was so much engaged in watching the occasional appearance of some trout in the water, and talking to the man about them, that he advanced but little. Whilst wandering on in this slow manner, they were again surprised, and Elizabeth's astonishment was quite equal to what it had been at first, by the sight of Mr Darcy approaching them, and at no great distance. The walk being here less sheltered than on the other side, allowed them to see him before they met. Elizabeth, however astonished, was at least more prepared for an interview than before, and resolved to appear and to speak with calmness, if he really intended to meet them. For a few moments, indeed, she felt that he would probably strike into some other path. This idea lasted while a turning in the walk concealed him from their view; the turning past, he was immediately before them. With a glance she saw, that he had lost none of his recent civility; and, to imitate his politeness, she began as they met to admire the beauty of the place; but she had not got beyond the words 'delightful', and 'charming', when some unlucky recollections obtruded, and she fancied that praise of Pemberley from her might be mischievously construed. Her colour changed, and she said no more.

Mrs Gardiner was standing a little behind; and on her pausing, he asked her if she would do him the honour of introducing him to her friends. This was a stroke of civility for which she was quite unprepared; and she could hardly suppress a smile at his being now seeking the acquaintance of some of those very people against whom his pride had revolted in his offer to herself. 'What will be his surprise,' thought she, 'when he knows who they are? He takes them now for people of fashion.'

The introduction, however, was immediately made; and as she named their relationship to herself, she stole a sly look at him, to see how he bore it, and was not without the expectation of his decamping as fast as he could from such disgraceful companions. That he was *surprised* by the connexion was evident; he sustained it, however, with fortitude, and, so far from going away, turned back with them, and entered into conversation with Mr Gardiner. Elizabeth could not but be pleased, could not but triumph. It was consoling that he should know she had some relations for whom there was no need to blush. She listened most attentively to all that passed between them, and gloried in every expression, every sentence of her uncle, which marked his intelligence, his taste, or his good manners.

The conversation soon turned upon fishing; and she heard Mr Darcy invite him, with the greatest civility, to fish there as often as he chose while he continued in the neighbourhood, offering at the same time to supply him with fishing tackle, and pointing out those parts of the stream where there was usually most sport. Mrs Gardiner, who was walking arm-in-arm with Elizabeth, gave her a look expressive of her wonder. Elizabeth said nothing, but it gratified her exceedingly; the compliment must be all for herself. Her astonishment, however, was extreme, and continually was she repeating, 'Why is he so altered? From what can it proceed? It cannot be for *me* – it cannot be for *my* sake that his manners are thus softened. My reproofs at Hunsford could not work such a change as this. It is impossible that he should still love me.'

After walking some time in this way, the two ladies in front, the two gentlemen behind, on resuming their places, after descending to the brink of the river for the better inspection of some curious water-plant, there chanced to be a little alteration. It originated in Mrs Gardiner, who, fatigued by the exercise of the morning, found Elizabeth's arm inadequate to her support, and consequently preferred her husband's. Mr Darcy took her place by her niece, and they walked on together. After a short silence, the lady first spoke. She wished him to know that she had been assured of his absence before she came to the place, and accordingly began by observing, that his arrival had been very unexpected, 'For your housekeeper,' she added, 'informed us that you would certainly not be here till tomorrow; and indeed, before we left Bakewell, we understood that you were not immediately expected in the country.' He acknowledged the truth of it all, and said that business with his steward had occasioned his coming forward a few hours before the rest of the party with whom he had been travelling. 'They will join me early tomorrow,' he continued, 'and among them are some who will claim an acquaintance with you – Mr Bingley and his sisters.'

Elizabeth answered only by a slight bow. Her thoughts were instantly driven back to the time when Mr Bingley's name had been last mentioned between them; and, if she might judge from his complexion, *his* mind was not very differently engaged.

'There is also one other person in the party,' he continued after a pause, 'who more particularly wishes to be known to you. Will you allow me, or do I ask too much, to introduce my sister to your acquaintance during your stay at Lambton?'

The surprise of such an application was great indeed; it was too great for her to know in what manner she acceded to it. She immediately felt that whatever desire Miss Darcy might have of being acquainted with her must be the work of her brother, and, without looking farther, it was satisfactory; it was gratifying to know that his resentment had not made him think really ill of her.

They now walked on in silence, each of them deep in thought. Elizabeth was not comfortable; that was impossible; but she was flattered and pleased. His wish of introducing his sister to her was a compliment of the highest kind. They soon outstripped the others, and when they had reached the carriage, Mr and Mrs Gardiner were half a quarter of a mile behind.

He then asked her to walk into the house – but she declared herself not tired, and they stood together on the lawn. At such a time, much might have been said, and silence was very awkward. She wanted to talk, but there seemed an embargo on every subject. At last she recollected that she had been travelling, and they talked of Matlock and Dovedale with great perseverance. Yet time and her aunt moved slowly – and her patience and her ideas were nearly worn out before the tête-à-tête was over. On Mr and Mrs Gardiner's coming up, they were all pressed to go into the house and take some refreshment; but this was declined, and they parted on each side with the utmost politeness. Mr Darcy handed the ladies into the carriage; and when it drove off, Elizabeth saw him walking slowly towards the house.

Jane Austen, *Pride and Prejudice* (1813)

Walking and Wooing: 'now or never'

Some minutes more passed, they moved still further away from the children and were quite alone. Varenka's heart beat so that she seemed to hear it, and she felt herself growing red and then pale and then red again.

To be the wife of a man like Koznyshev after her difficult life with Madame Stahl seemed to her the height of bliss. Besides, she was almost sure she loved him, and now in a moment it must be decided. She was frightened, frightened of what he might or might not say. 'He must make his decision now or never.'

Koznyshev also felt this. Everything – Varenka's look, her blush, her downcast eyes – betrayed painful expectation. He saw it and was sorry for her. He even felt that to say nothing now would be to offend her. His mind went rapidly over all the arguments in favour of his decision. He repeated to himself the words with which he had intended to propose; but instead of those words some unexpected thought caused him to say:

'What difference is there between the white boleti and the birch-tree variety?'

Varenka's lips trembled with emotion when she replied:

'There is hardly any difference in the tops, but only in the stems.'

And as soon as those words were spoken, both he and she understood that all was over, and that what ought to have been said would not be said, and their excitement, having reached its climax, began to subside.

'The stem of the birch-tree's boletus reminds one of a dark man's beard two days old,' remarked Koznyshev calmly.

'Yes, that's true,' remarked Varenka with a smile, and involuntarily their walk had changed.

Leo Tolstoy, *Anna Karenina* (1873–7)
Translated by Constance Garnett

'Are you happier?' she asked, wistfully.

'Much better, and I was rather far gone.'

She nestled against him. He felt her all soft and warm, she was the rich, lovely substance of his being. The warmth and motion of her walk suffused through him wonderfully.

'I'm so glad if I help you,' she said.

'Yes,' he answered. 'There's nobody else could do it, if you wouldn't.'

'That is true,' she said to herself, with a thrill of strange, fatal elation.

As they walked, he seemed to lift her nearer and nearer to himself, till she moved upon the firm vehicle of his body.

He was so strong, so sustaining, and he could not be opposed. She drifted along in a wonderful interfusion of physical motion, down the dark, blowy hillside. Far across shone the little yellow lights of Beldover, many of them, spread in a thick patch on another dark hill. But he and she were walking in perfect, isolated darkness, outside the world.

'But how much do you care for me!' came her voice, almost querulous. 'You see, I don't know, I don't understand!'

'How much!' His voice rang with a painful elation. 'I don't know either – but everything.' He was startled by his own declaration. It was true. So he stripped himself of every safeguard, in making this admission to her. He cared everything for her – she was everything.

'But I can't believe it,' said her low voice, amazed, trembling. She was trembling with doubt and exultance. This was the thing she wanted to hear, only this. Yet now she heard it, heard the strange clapping vibration of truth in his voice as he said it, she could not believe. She could not believe – she did not believe. Yet she believed, triumphantly, with fatal exultance.

'Why not?' he said. 'Why don't you believe it? It's true. It is true, as we stand at this moment –' he stood still with her in the wind; 'I care for nothing on earth, or in heaven, outside this spot where we are. And it isn't my own presence I care about, it is all yours. I'd sell my soul a hundred times – but I couldn't bear not to have you here. I couldn't bear to be alone. My brain would burst. It is true.' He drew her closer to him, with definite movement.

'No,' she murmured, afraid. Yet this was what she wanted. Why did she so lose courage?

They resumed their strange walk.

They were such strangers – and yet they were so frightfully, unthinkably near. It was like a madness. Yet it was what she wanted, it was what she wanted. They had descended the hill, and now they were coming to the square arch where the road passed under the colliery railway. The arch, Gudrun knew, had walls of squared stone, mossy on one side with water that trickled down, dry on the other side. She had stood under it to hear the train rumble thundering over the logs overhead. And she knew that under this dark and lonely bridge the young colliers stood in the darkness with their sweethearts, in rainy weather. And so she wanted to stand under the bridge with her sweetheart, and be kissed under the bridge in the invisible darkness. Her steps dragged as she drew near.

So, under the bridge, they came to a standstill, and he lifted her upon his breast. His body vibrated taut and powerful as he closed upon her and crushed her, breathless and dazed and destroyed, crushed her upon his breast. Ah, it was terrible, and perfect. Under this bridge, the colliers pressed their lovers to their breast. And now, under the bridge, the master of them all pressed her to himself? And how much more powerful and terrible was his embrace than theirs, how much more concentrated and supreme his love was, than theirs in the same sort! She felt she would swoon, die, under the vibrating, inhuman tension of his arms and his body – she would pass away. Then the unthinkable high vibration slackened and became more undulating. He slackened and drew her with him to stand with his back to the wall. She was almost unconscious.

'This is worth everything,' he said, in a strange, penetrating voice.

So she relaxed, and seemed to melt, to flow into him, as if she were some infinitely warm and precious suffusion filling into his veins, like an intoxicant. Her arms were round his neck, he kissed her and held her perfectly suspended, she was all slack and flowing into him, and he was the firm, strong cup that receives the wine of her life.

Till she seemed to swoon, gradually her mind went, and she passed away, everything in her was melted down and fluid, and she lay still, become contained by him, sleeping in him as lightning sleeps in a pure, soft stone. So she was passed away and gone in him, and he was perfected.

When she opened her eyes again, and saw the patch of lights in the distance, it seemed to her strange that the world still existed, that she was standing under the bridge resting her head on Gerald's breast. Gerald – who was he? He was the exquisite adventure, the desirable unknown to her.

'You are so beautiful,' she murmured in her throat.

He wondered, and was suspended. But she felt him quiver, and she came down involuntarily nearer upon him. He could not help himself. Her fingers had him under their power. The fathomless, fathomless desire they could evoke in him was deeper than death, where he had no choice. But she knew now, and it was enough.

For the time, her soul was destroyed with the exquisite shock of his invisible fluid lightning. She knew. And this knowledge was a death from which she must recover. Enough now – enough for the time being. And even he was glad to be checked, rebuked, held back. For to desire is better than to possess, the finality of the end was dreaded as deeply as it was desired.

They walked on towards the town, towards where the lamps threaded singly, at long intervals down the dark high-road of the valley. They came at length to the gate of the drive.

'Don't come any further,' she said.

'You'd rather I didn't?' he asked, relieved. He did not want to go up the public streets with her, his soul all naked and alight as it was.

'Much rather – goodnight.' She held out her hand. He grasped it, then touched the perilous, potent fingers with his lips.

'Goodnight,' he said. 'Tomorrow.'

And they parted.

D.H. Lawrence, *Women in Love* (1921)

I Nauseate Walking

SIR WILFUL   Yes, I made bold to see, to come and know if that how you were disposed to fetch a walk this evening. If so be that I might not be troublesome, I would have sought a walk with you.

MILLAMANT   A walk? What then?

SIR WILFUL   Nay nothing… only for the walk's sake, that's all –

MILLAMANT   I nauseate walking, 'tis a country diversion. I loathe the country and everything that relates to it.

William Congreve, *The Way of the World* (1700)

Discovery…

Thursday, the thirty-first of August, was one of a series of days during which snug houses were stifling, and when cool draughts were treats; when cracks appeared in clayey gardens, and were called 'earthquakes' by apprehensive children; when loose spokes were discovered in the wheels of carts and carriages; and when stinging insects haunted the air, the earth, and every drop of water that was to be found…

It was about eleven o'clock on this day that Mrs Yeobright started across the heath towards her son's house, to do her best in getting reconciled with him and Eustacia, in conformity with her words to the reddleman. She had hoped to be well advanced in her walk before the heat of the day was at its highest, but after setting out she found that this was not to be done. The sun had branded the whole heath with his mark, even the purple heath-flowers having put on a brownness under the dry blazes of the few preceding days. Every valley was filled with air like that of a kiln, and the clean quartz sand of the winter water-courses, which formed summer paths, had undergone a species of in-cineration since the drought had set in.

In cool, fresh weather Mrs Yeobright would have found no inconvenience in walking to Alderworth. But the present torrid attack made the journey a heavy undertaking for a woman past middle age; and at the end of the third mile she wished that she had hired Fairway to drive her a portion at least of the distance. But from the point at which she had arrived it was as easy to reach Clym's house as to get home again. So she went on, the air around her pulsating silently, and oppressing the earth with lassi-tude. She looked at the sky overhead, and saw that the sapphirine hue of the zenith in spring and early summer had been replaced by a metallic violet…

Mrs Yeobright had never before been to her son's house, and its exact position was unknown to her. She tried one ascending path and another, and found that they led her astray. Retracing her steps, she came again to an open level, where she perceived at a distance a man at work. She went towards him and inquired the way.

The labourer pointed out the direction, and added, 'Do you see that furze-cutter, ma'am, going up that footpath yond?'

Mrs Yeobright strained her eyes, and at last said that she did perceive him.

'Well, if you follow him you can make no mistake. He's going to the same place, ma'am.'

She followed the figure indicated. He appeared of a russet hue, not more distinguishable from the scene around him than the green caterpillar from the leaf it feeds on. His progress when actually walking was more rapid than Mrs Yeobright's; but she was enabled to keep at an equable distance from him by his habit of stopping whenever he came to a brake of brambles, where he paused awhile. On coming in her turn to each of these spots she found half a dozen long limp brambles which he had cut from the bush during his halt and laid out straight beside the path. They were evidently intended for furze-faggot bonds which he meant to collect on his return.

The silent being who thus occupied himself seemed to be of no more account in life than an insect. He appeared as a mere parasite of the heath, fretting its surface in his daily labour as a moth frets a garment, entirely engrossed with its products, having no knowledge of anything in the world but fern, furze, heath, lichens, and moss.

The furze-cutter was so absorbed in the business of his journey that he never turned his head; and his leather-legged and gauntleted form at length became to her as nothing more than a moving handpost to show her the way. Suddenly she was attracted to his individuality by observing peculiarities in his walk. It was a gait she had seen somewhere before; and the gait revealed the man to her, as the gait of Ahimaaz in the distant plain made him known to the watchman of the king. 'His walk is exactly as my husband's used to be,' she said; and then the thought burst upon her that the furze-cutter was her son.

She was scarcely able to familiarise herself with this strange reality. She had been told that Clym was in the habit of cutting furze, but she had supposed that he occupied himself with the labour only at odd times, by way of useful pastime. Yet she now beheld him as a furze-cutter and nothing more – wearing the regulation dress of the craft, and thinking the regulation thoughts, to judge by his motions. Planning a dozen hasty schemes for at once preserving him and Eustacia from this mode of life, she throbbingly followed the way, and saw him enter his own door.

At one side of Clym's house was a knoll, and on the top of the knoll a clump of fir trees so highly thrust up into the sky that their foliage from a distance appeared as a black spot in the air above the crown of the hill. On reaching this place Mrs Yeobright felt distressingly agitated, weary, and unwell. She ascended, and sat down under their shade to recover herself, and to consider how best to break the ground with Eustacia, so as not to irritate a woman underneath whose apparent indolence lurked passions even stronger and more active than her own.

The trees beneath which she sat were singularly battered, rude, and wild, and for a few minutes Mrs Yeobright dismissed thoughts of her own storm-broken and exhausted state to con-template theirs… Some were blasted and split as if by lightning, black stains as from fire marking their sides, while the ground at their feet was strewn with dead fir-needles and heaps of cones blown down in the gales of past years. The place was called the Devil's Bellows, and it was only necessary to come there on a March or November night to discover the forcible reasons for that name. On the present heated afternoon, when no percept-ible wind was blowing, the trees kept up a perpetual moan which one could hardly believe to be caused by the air.

Here she sat for twenty minutes or more ere she could summon resolution to go down to the door, her courage being lowered to zero by her physical lassitude. To any other person than a mother it might have seemed a little humiliating that she, the elder of the two women, should be the first to make advances. But Mrs Yeobright had well considered all that, and she only thought how best to make her visit appear to Eustacia not abject but wise.

From her elevated position the exhausted woman could per-ceive the roof of the house below, and the garden and the whole enclosure of the little domicile. And now, at the moment of rising, she saw a second man approaching the gate. His manner was peculiar, hesitating, and not that of a person come on business or by invitation. He surveyed the house with interest, and then walked round and scanned the outer boundary of the garden, as one might have done had it been the birthplace of Shakespeare, the prison of Mary Stuart, or the Château of Hougomont. After passing round and again reaching the gate he went in. Mrs Yeobright was vexed at this, having reckoned on finding her son and his wife by themselves; but a moment's thought showed her that the presence of an acquaintance would take off the awkwardness of her first appearance in the house, by confining the talk to general matters until she had begun to feel comfortable with them.

She came down the hill to the gate, and looked into the hot garden...

Thomas Hardy, *The Return of the Native* (1878)

A Family Outing

Instead of taking us home at once, my father, in his thirst for personal distinction, would lead us on a long walk round by the Calvary, which my mother's utter incapacity for taking her bearings, or even for knowing which road she might be on, made her regard as a triumph of his strategic genius. Sometimes we would go as far as the viaduct, which began to stride on its long legs of stone at the railway station, and to me typified all the wretchedness of exile beyond the last outposts of civilization, because every year, as we came down from Paris, we would be warned to take special care, when we got to Combray, not to miss the station, to be ready before the train stopped, since it would start again in two minutes and proceed across the viaduct, out of the lands of Christendom, of which Combray, to me, represented the farthest limit. We would return by the Boulevard de la Gare, which contained the most attractive villas in the town... From gates far apart the watchdogs, awakened by our steps in the silence, would set up an antiphonal barking, as I still hear them bark, in the evenings, and it is in their custody... that the Boulevard de la Gare must have taken refuge, for wherever I may be, as soon as they begin their alternate challenge and acceptance, I can see it all again with its lime trees, and its pavements glistening beneath the moon.

Suddenly my father would bring us to a standstill and ask my mother – 'Where are we?' Utterly worn out by the walk but still proud of her husband, she would lovingly confess that she had not the least idea. He would shrug his shoulders and laugh, and then, as though it had slipped, with his latchkey, from his waist-coat pocket, he would point out to us, where it stood before our eyes, the back gate of our own garden, which had come, hand in hand, with the familiar corner of the Rue de Saint-Esprit, to await us, to greet us at the end of our wanderings over paths unknown. My mother would murmur admiringly, 'You really are wonderful.' And from that instant I had not to take another step. The ground moved forward under my feet in that garden where, for so long, my actions had ceased to require any control, or even attention, from my will. Custom came to take me in her arms, carried me all the way to my bed, and laid me down there like a little child.

Marcel Proust, *Swann's Way* (1913)
Translated by C.K. Scott Moncrieff

Little Feet

'Wait for me, Isa-bel! Kezia, wait for me!'

There was poor little Lottie, left behind again, because she found it so fearfully hard to get over the stile by herself. When she stood on the first step her knees began to wobble; she grasped the post. Then you had to put one leg over. But which leg? She never could decide. And when she did finally put one leg over with a sort of stamp of despair – then the feeling was awful. She was half in the paddock still and half in the tussock grass. She clutched the post desperately and lifted up her voice. 'Wait for me!'

'No, don't you wait for her, Kezia!' said Isabel. 'She's such a little silly. She's always making a fuss. Come on!' And she tugged Kezia's jersey. 'You can use my bucket if you come with me,' she said kindly. 'It's bigger than yours.' But Kezia couldn't leave Lottie all by herself. She ran back to her. By this time, Lottie was very red in the face and breathing heavily.

'Here, put your other foot over,' said Kezia.

'Where?'

Lottie looked down at Kezia as if from a mountain height.

'Here where my hand is.' Kezia patted the place.

'Oh, *there* do you mean!' Lottie gave a deep sigh and put the second foot over.

'Now – sort of turn round and sit down and slide,' said Kezia.

'But there's nothing to sit down *on*, Kezia,' said Lottie.

She managed it at last, and once it was over she shook herself and began to beam.

'I'm getting better at climbing over stiles, aren't I, Kezia?'

Lottie's was a very hopeful nature.

Katherine Mansfield, 'At The Bay' (1922)

Marching Types

'Take out your scent-bottles, the sweat of the people is passing by!' murmured Négrel, who, in spite of his republican convictions, liked to make fun of the populace when he was with the ladies.

But his witticism was carried away in the hurricane of gestures and cries. The women had appeared, nearly a thousand of them, with outspread hair dishevelled by running, the naked skin appearing through their rags, the nakedness of females weary with giving birth to starvelings. A few held their little ones in their arms, raising them and shaking them like banners of mourning and vengeance. Others, who were younger with the swollen breasts of amazons, brandished sticks; while frightful old women were yelling so loudly that the cords of their fleshless necks seemed to be breaking.

And then the men came up, two thousand madmen – trammers, pikemen, menders – a compact mass which rolled along like a single block in confused serried rank so that it was impossible to distinguish their faded trousers or ragged woollen jackets, all effaced in the same earthy uniformity. Their eyes were burning, and one only distinguished the holes of black mouths singing the Marseillaise. The stanzas were lost in a confused roar, accompanied by the clang of sabots over the hard earth. Above their heads, amid the bristling iron bars, an axe passed by, carried erect; and this single axe, which seemed to be the standard of the band, showed in the clear air the sharp profile of a guillotine-blade.

'What atrocious faces!' stammered Madame Hennebeau.

Négrel said between his teeth, 'Devil take me if I can recognise one of them! Where do the bandits spring from?'

And in fact anger, hunger, these two months of suffering and this enraged helter-skelter through the pits had lengthened the placid faces of the Montsou colliers into the muzzles of wild beasts. At this moment the sun was setting. Its last rays of sombre purple cast a gleam of blood over the plain. The road seemed to be full of blood. Men and women continued to rush by, bloody as butchers in the midst of slaughter.

'Oh! superb!' whispered Lucie and Jeanne, stirred in their artistic tastes by the beautiful horror of it.

They were frightened, however, and drew back close to Madame Hennebeau, who was leaning on a trough. She was frozen at the thought that a glance between the planks of that disjointed door might suffice to murder them. Négrel also, who was usually brave, felt himself grow pale, seized by a terror that was superior to his will, the terror which comes from the unknown. Cécile, in the hay, no longer stirred; and the others, in spite of the wish to turn away their eyes, could not do so. They were compelled to gaze.

It was the red vision of the revolution, which would one day inevitably carry them all away, on some bloody evening at the end of the century. Yes, some evening the people, unbridled at last, would thus gallop along the roads, making the blood of the middle class flow, parading severed heads and sprinkling gold from disembowelled coffers. The women would yell, the men would have those wolf-like jaws open to bite. Yes, the same rags, the same thunder of great sabots, the same terrible troop, with dirty skins and tainted breath, sweeping away the old world beneath an overflowing flood of barbarians. Fires would flame. They would not leave standing one stone of the towns. They would return to the savage life of the woods, after the great rut, the great feast-day, when the poor in one night would emaciate the wives and empty the cellars of the rich. There would be nothing left, not a sou of the great fortunes, not a title-deed of properties acquired; until the day dawned when a new earth would perhaps spring up once more. Yes, it was these things which were passing along the road. It was the force of nature herself, and they were receiving the terrible wind of it in their faces.

A great cry arose, dominating the Marseillaise, 'Bread! bread! bread!'

Lucie and Jeanne pressed themselves against Madame Hennebeau, who was almost fainting; while Négrel placed himself before them as though to protect them by his body. Was the old social order cracking this very evening? And what they saw immediately after completed their stupefaction. The band had almost passed by, there were only a few stragglers left, when

Mouquette came up. She was delaying, watching the bourgeois at their garden gates or the windows of their houses. And whenever she saw them, she showed them what for her was the climax of contempt. Suddenly she raised her skirts, bent her back, and showed her enormous buttocks, naked beneath the last rays of the sun. There was nothing obscene in those fierce buttocks – and nobody laughed.

Everything disappeared. The flood rolled on to Montsou along the turns of the road, between the low houses streaked with bright colours. The carriage was drawn out of the yard, but the coachman would not take it upon him to convey back madame and the young ladies without delay; the strikers occupied the street.

And the worst was, there was no other road.

Emile Zola, *Germinal* (1885)
Translated by Havelock Ellis

Quest

The great granite tunnel had the appearance of a labyrinth. Its direction was in general towards the south-west. And my uncle made several pauses in order to consult his compass.

The gallery began to run downwards in a horizontal direction, with about two inches of fall in every furlong. The murmuring stream flowed quietly at our feet. I could only compare it to some familiar spirit, guiding us through the earth, and I dabbled my fingers in its tepid water, which sang like a naiad as we progressed. My good humour began to assume a mythological character.

My uncle began to complain of the horizontal character of the road. His route, he found, began to be prolonged, instead of 'sliding down the celestial ray', according to his expression. But we had no choice; and as long as our road led towards the center, there was no reason to complain. From time to time the slopes were much greater, the naiad sang more loudly, and we began to dip downwards in earnest. As yet I felt no painful sensation. I hadn't got over the excitement of the discovery of water.

That day, and the next, we did a considerable amount of horizontal and very little vertical travelling.

On Friday evening, the tenth of July, according to our estimation, we ought to have been thirty leagues to the south-east of Reykjavik, and about two leagues and a half deep. We now received a rather startling surprise. Under our feet there opened a horrible well. My uncle was so delighted he clapped his hands. He saw how steep and sharp was the descent.

'Ah, ah!' he cried, 'this takes us a long way. Look at the projections of the rock. Hah!' he exclaimed, 'it's a fearful staircase!'

Hans, however, who in all our troubles had never given up the ropes, took care to dispose of them in order to prevent any accidents.

Our descent then began.

This well had a narrow opening in the massive granite, known as a fissure. The contraction of the terrestrial scaffolding, when it suddenly cooled, had been the cause. If it had served as a kind of funnel, through which passed the eruptive masses vomited by Sneffels, then I was at a loss to explain how it had left no mark. We were, in fact, descending a spiral, something like those winding staircases in modern houses.

We were compelled every quarter of an hour to sit down and rest our legs. Our calves ached. We sat on a projecting rock with our legs hanging over, and gossiped while we ate a mouthful and drank from the warm running stream, which had not deserted us.

In this curiously shaped fissure the Hansbach had become a cascade to the detriment of its size. It was still, however, sufficient for our needs. Besides we knew that, as soon as the declivity ceased to be abrupt, the stream would resume its peaceful course.

At this moment it reminded me of my uncle, his impatience and rage, and when it flowed more peacefully, I pictured the placidity of the Icelandic guide.

During the whole of two days, the sixth and seventh of July, we followed the extraordinary spiral staircase of the fissure, penetrating two leagues farther into the crust of the earth, which put us five leagues below the level of the sea. On the eighth day however, at twelve o'clock, the fissure assumed a more gentle slope, still trending in a south-east direction.

The road became more easy, at the same time dreadfully monotonous. It would have been difficult for matters to have turned out otherwise. Our peculiar journey had no chance of being altered by landscape and scenery.

At length, on Wednesday the fifteenth, we were actually seven leagues (twenty-one miles) under the surface of the earth, and fifty leagues distant from the mountain of Sneffels. We were very tired. But our health had resisted all suffering, and was in a most satisfactory state. Our traveller's box of medicaments had not been opened.

My uncle was careful to note, every hour, the indications of the compass, of the manometer, of the thermometer, all which he afterwards published in his elaborate philosophical and scientific account of our voyage. He was able to give an exact relation of the situation. When he informed me we were fifty leagues in a horizontal direction distant from our starting point, I could not suppress an exclamation.

'What's the matter now?' cried my uncle.

'Nothing very important... only an idea has entered my head.'

'Well, out with it, my boy.'

'If your calculations are correct we are no longer under Iceland.'

'You think so?'

'We can very easily find out,' I replied, pulling out a map and compasses.

'You see,' I said, after careful measurement, 'I am not mistaken. We are far beyond Cape Portland, and those fifty leagues to the south-east will take us into the open sea.'

'Under the open sea,' cried my uncle, rubbing his hands with a delighted air.

'Yes,' I cried… 'old Ocean flows over our heads!'

'Well, my dear boy, what can be more natural! Do you know in the neighborhood of Newcastle there are coal mines that have been worked far out under the sea?'

Now my worthy uncle, the Professor, regarded this discovery as a simple fact. But to me the idea was by no means a pleasant one. And yet when one thought the matter over – what mattered if the plains and mountains of Iceland were suspended over our devoted heads, or the mighty billows of the Atlantic Ocean? The whole question rested on the solidity of the granite roof above us. However, I soon got used to the passage now level, now running down, always to the south-east.

It kept going deeper and deeper into the profound abysses of Mother Earth.

Three days later, on the eighteenth day of July, on a Saturday, we reached a vast grotto. Here my uncle paid Hans his usual six-dollars, and it was decided that the next day would be a day of rest.

Jules Verne, *A Journey To the Centre of the Earth* (1864)
Translated by Griffith and Farran

Nightwalking: Confusion

Jupiter was setting in the depths. The child stared with great bewilderment at this great star, which terrified her. A cold wind was blowing from the plain. Great boughs lifted themselves in frightful wise. Slender and misshapen bushes whistled in the clearings.

The darkness was confusing. Man requires light. Whoever buries himself in the opposite of day feels his heart contract. When the eye sees black, the heart sees trouble. In an eclipse in the night, in the sooty opacity, there is anxiety even for the stoutest of hearts. No one walks alone at night without trembling.

Cossette was conscious she was seized by that black enormity. Then by some instinct she began to count out aloud – one, two, three, four, and so on up to ten, in order to escape from that singular state which she did not understand. This restored her to a true perception of the things about her. She rose. She had but one thought about now – to flee at full speed, across the fields, to the house, to the windows, to the lighted candles...

Victor Hugo, *Les Misérables* (1862)
Translated by Isabel F. Hapgood

Nightwalking: Melodrama

As he turned more fully to the light of a lamp above him, I saw that he was a young, distinguished, and handsome man. He might be a lord, for anything I knew. Nature had made him good enough for a prince, I thought. His face was very pleasant; he looked high but not arrogant, manly but not overbearing. I was turning away, in the deep consciousness of all absence of claim to look for further help from such a one as he.

'Was all your money in your trunk?' he asked, stopping me.

How thankful was I to be able to answer with truth, 'No. I have enough in my purse' (for I had near twenty francs) 'to keep me at a quiet inn till the day after tomorrow; but I am quite a stranger in Villette, and don't know the streets and the inns.'

'I can give you the address of such an inn as you want,' said he; 'and it is not far off: with my direction you will easily find it.'

He tore a leaf from his pocket-book, wrote a few words and gave it to me. I *did* think him kindly; and as to distrusting him, or his advice, or his address, I should almost as soon have thought of distrusting the Bible. There was goodness in his countenance, and honour in his bright eyes.

'Your shortest way will be to follow the boulevard and cross the park,' he continued; 'but it is too late and too dark for a woman to go through the park alone; I will step with you thus far.'

He moved on, and I followed him, through the darkness and the small soaking rain. The boulevard was all deserted, its path miry, the water dripping from its trees; the park was black as midnight. In the double gloom of trees and fog, I could not see my guide; I could only follow his tread. Not the least fear had I: I believe I would have followed that frank tread, through continual night, to the world's end.

'Now,' said he, when the park was traversed, 'you will go along this broad street till you come to steps; two lamps will show you where they are: these steps you will descend: a narrower street lies below; following that, at the bottom you will find your inn. They speak English there, so your difficulties are now pretty well over. Goodnight.'

'Goodnight, sir,' said I, 'accept my sincerest thanks.' And we parted.

The remembrance of his countenance, which I am sure wore a light not unbenignant to the friendless – the sound in my ear of his voice, which spoke a nature chivalric to the needy and feeble, as well as the youthful and fair – were a sort of cordial to me long after. He was a true young English gentleman.

On I went, hurrying fast through a magnificent street and square, with the grandest houses round, and amidst them the huge outline of more than one overbearing pile; which might be palace or church – I could not tell. Just as I passed a portico, two mustachioed men came suddenly from behind the pillars; they were smoking cigars: their dress implied pretensions to the rank of gentlemen, but, poor things! they were very plebeian in soul. They spoke with insolence, and, fast as I walked, they kept pace with me a long way. At last I met a sort of patrol, and my dreaded hunters were turned from the pursuit; but they had driven me beyond my reckoning: when I could collect my faculties, I no longer knew where I was; the staircase I must long since have passed. Puzzled, out of breath, all my pulses throbbing in inevitable agitation, I knew not where to turn. It was terrible to think of again encountering those bearded, sneering simpletons; yet the ground must be retraced, and the steps sought out.

I came at last to an old and worn flight, and, taking it for granted that this must be the one indicated, I descended them. The street into which they led was indeed narrow, but it contained no inn. On I wandered. In a very quiet and comparatively clean and well-paved street, I saw a light burning over the door of a rather large house, loftier by a story than those round it. *This* might be the inn at last. I hastened on: my knees now trembled under me: I was getting quite exhausted.

No inn was this. A brass-plate embellished the great *porte-cochère*: '*Pensionnat de Demoiselles*' was the inscription.

Charlotte Brontë, *Villette* (1853)

Nightwalking: Dread

Young Goodman Brown came forth at sunset into the street of Salem village; but put his head back, after crossing the threshold, to exchange a parting kiss with his young wife. And Faith, as the wife was aptly named, thrust her own pretty head into the street, letting the wind play with the pink ribbons of her cap while she called to Goodman Brown.

'Dearest heart,' whispered she, softly and rather sadly, when her lips were close to his ear, 'prithee put off your journey until sunrise and sleep in your own bed tonight. A lone woman is troubled with such dreams and such thoughts that she's afeard of herself sometimes. Pray tarry with me this night, dear husband, of all nights in the year.'

'My love and my Faith,' replied young Goodman Brown, 'of all nights in the year, this one night must I tarry away from thee. My journey, as thou callest it, forth and back again, must needs be done 'twixt now and sunrise. What, my sweet, pretty wife, dost thou doubt me already, and we but three months married?'

'Then God bless you!' said Faith, with the pink ribbons, 'and may you find all well when you come back.'

'Amen!' cried Goodman Brown. 'Say thy prayers, dear Faith, and go to bed at dusk, and no harm will come to thee.'

So they parted, and the young man pursued his way until, being about to turn the corner by the meeting house, he looked back and saw the head of Faith still peeping after him with a melancholy air, in spite of her pink ribbons.

'Poor little Faith!' thought he, for his heart smote him. 'What a wretch am I to leave her on such an errand! She talks of dreams, too. Methought as she spoke there was trouble in her face, as if a dream had warned her what work is to be done tonight. But no, no; 'twould kill her to think it. She's a blessed angel on earth; and after this one night I'll cling to her skirts and follow her to heaven.'

With this excellent resolve for the future, Goodman Brown felt himself justified in making more haste on his present evil purpose. He had taken a dreary road, darkened by all the gloomiest trees of the forest, which barely stood aside to let the narrow path creep through, and closed immediately behind. It was all as lonely as could be; and there is this peculiarity in such a solitude, that the traveller knows not who may be concealed by the innumerable trunks and the thick boughs overhead; so that with lonely footsteps he may yet be passing through an unseen multitude.

'There may be a devilish Indian behind every tree,' said Goodman Brown to himself; and he glanced fearfully behind him as he added, 'What if the Devil himself should be at my very elbow!'

His head being turned back, he passed a crook of the road, and, looking forward again, beheld the figure of a man, in grave and decent attire, seated at the foot of an old tree. He arose at Goodman Brown's approach and walked onward side by side with him.

'You are late, Goodman Brown,' said he. 'The clock of the Old South was striking as I came through Boston, and that is full fifteen minutes gone.'

'Faith kept me back awhile,' replied the young man, with a tremor in his voice, caused by the sudden appearance of his companion, though not wholly unexpected.

It was now deep dusk in the forest, and deepest in that part of it where these two were journeying. As nearly as could be discerned, the second traveller was about fifty years old, apparently in the same rank of life as Goodman Brown, and bearing a considerable resemblance to him, though perhaps more in expression than features. Still they might have been taken for father and son. And yet, though the elder person was as simply clad as the younger and as simple in manner too, he had an indescribable air of one who knew the world, and who would not have felt abashed at the governor's dinner table or in King William's court, were it possible that his affairs should call him thither. But the only thing about him that could be fixed upon as remarkable was his staff, which bore the likeness of a great black snake, so curiously wrought that it might almost be seen to twist and wriggle itself like a living serpent. This, of course, must have been an ocular deception, assisted by the uncertain light.

'Come, Goodman Brown,' cried his fellow-traveller, 'this is a dull pace for the beginning of a journey. Take my staff, if you are so soon weary.'

'Friend,' said the other, exchanging his slow pace for a full stop, 'having kept covenant by meeting thee here, it is my purpose now to return whence I came. I have scruples touching the matter thou wot'st of.'

'Sayest thou so?' replied he of the serpent, smiling apart. 'Let us walk on, nevertheless, reasoning as we go; and if I convince thee not, thou shalt turn back. We are but a little way in the forest yet.'

'Too far! too far!' exclaimed the goodman, unconsciously resuming his walk. 'My father never went into the woods on such an errand, nor his father before him. We have been a race of honest men and good Christians since the days of the martyrs; and shall I be the first of the name of Brown that ever took this path and kept –'

'Such company, thou wouldst say,' observed the elder person, interpreting his pause. 'Well said, Goodman Brown! I have been as well acquainted with your family as with ever a one among the Puritans; and that's no trifle to say. I helped your grandfather, the constable, when he lashed the Quaker woman so smartly through the streets of Salem; and it was I that brought your father a pitch-pine knot, kindled at my own hearth, to set fire to an Indian village, in King Philip's war. They were my good friends both; and many a pleasant walk have we had along this path, and returned merrily after midnight. I would fain be friends with you for their sake.'

'If it be as thou sayest,' replied Goodman Brown, 'I marvel they never spoke of these matters; or, verily, I marvel not, seeing that the least rumor of the sort would have driven them from New England. We are a people of prayer, and good works to boot, and abide no such wickedness.'

'Wickedness or not,' said the traveler with the twisted staff, 'I have a very general acquaintance here in New England. The deacons of many a church have drunk the communion wine with me; the selectmen of divers towns make me their chairman; and a majority of the Great and General Court are firm supporters of my interest. The governor and I, too – but these are state secrets.'

'Can this be so?' cried Goodman Brown, with a stare of amazement at his undisturbed companion. 'Howbeit, I have nothing to do with the governor and council; they have their own ways, and are no rule for a simple husbandman like me. But, were I to go on with thee, how should I meet the eye of that good old man, our minister, at Salem village? Oh, his voice would make me tremble both Sabbath day and lecture day!'

Thus far the elder traveler had listened with due gravity; but now burst into a fit of irrepressible mirth, shaking himself so violently that his snake-like staff actually seemed to wriggle in sympathy.

'Ha! ha! ha!' shouted he again and again; then composing himself, 'Well, go on, Goodman Brown, go on; but, prithee, don't kill me with laughing.'

'Well, then, to end the matter at once,' said Goodman Brown, considerably nettled, 'there is my wife, Faith. It would break her dear little heart, and I'd rather break my own.'

'Nay, if that be the case,' answered the other, 'e'en go thy ways, Goodman Brown. I would not for twenty old women like the one hobbling before us that Faith should come to any harm.'

As he spoke, he pointed his staff at a female figure on the path, in whom Goodman Brown recognized a very pious and exemplary dame, who had taught him his catechism in youth, and was still his moral and spiritual adviser, jointly with the minister and Deacon Gookin.

'A marvel, truly, that Goody Cloyse should be so far in the wilderness at nightfall,' said he. 'But, with your leave, friend, I shall take a cut through the woods until we have left this Christian woman behind. Being a stranger to you, she might ask whom I was consorting with and whither I was going.'

'Be it so,' said his fellow-traveller. 'Betake you to the woods, and let me keep the path.'

Accordingly the young man turned aside, but took care to watch his companion, who advanced softly along the road until he had come within a staff's length of the old dame. She, meanwhile, was making the best of her way, with singular speed for so aged a woman, and mumbling some indistinct words – a prayer, doubtless – as she went. The traveler put forth his staff and touched her withered neck with what seemed the serpent's tail.

'The Devil!' screamed the pious old lady.

'Then Goody Cloyse knows her old friend?' observed the traveler, confronting her and leaning on his writhing stick.

'Ah, forsooth, and is it your worship indeed?' cried the good dame. 'Yea, truly is it, and in the very image of my old gossip, Goodman Brown, the grandfather of the silly fellow that now is. But – would your worship believe it? – my broomstick hath strangely disappeared, stolen, as I suspect, by that unhanged witch, Goody Cory, and that, too, when I was all anointed with the juice of smallage, and cinquefoil, and wolf's-bane –'

'Mingled with fine wheat and the fat of a new-born babe,' said the shape of old Goodman Brown.

'Ah, your worship knows the recipe,' cried the old lady, cackling aloud. 'So, as I was saying, being all ready for the meeting, and no horse to ride on, I made up my mind to foot it; for they tell me there is a nice young man to be taken into communion tonight. But now your good worship will lend me your arm, and we shall be there in a twinkling.'

'That can hardly be,' answered her friend. 'I may not spare you my arm, Goody Cloyse; but here is my staff, if you will.'

So saying, he threw it down at her feet, where, perhaps, it assumed life, being one of the rods which its owner had formerly lent to the Egyptian magi. Of this fact, however, Goodman Brown could not take cognizance. He had cast up his eyes in astonishment, and, looking down again, beheld neither Goody Cloyse nor the serpentine staff, but his fellow-traveler alone, who waited for him as calmly as if nothing had happened.

'That old woman taught me my catechism,' said the young man, and there was a world of meaning in this simple comment.

They continued to walk onward, while the elder traveler exhorted his companion to make good speed and persevere in the path. As they went, he plucked a branch of maple to serve for a walking stick, and began to strip it of the twigs and little boughs, which were wet with evening dew. The moment his fingers touched them they became strangely withered and dried up as with a week's sunshine. Thus the pair proceeded, at a good free pace, until suddenly, in a gloomy hollow of the road, Goodman Brown sat himself down on the stump of a tree and refused to go any farther.

'Friend,' said he, 'my mind is made up. Not another step will I budge on this errand. What if a wretched old woman do choose to go to the Devil when I thought she was going to heaven: is that any reason why I should quit my dear Faith and go after her?'

'You will think better of this by and by,' said his acquaintance. 'Sit here and rest yourself awhile; and when you feel like moving again, there is my staff to help you along.'

Without more words, he threw his companion the maple stick, and was as speedily out of sight as if he had vanished into the deepening gloom. The young man sat a few moments by the roadside, applauding himself greatly, and thinking with how clear a conscience he should meet the minister in his morning walk, nor shrink from the eye of good old Deacon Gookin. And what calm sleep would be his that very night, which was to have been spent so wickedly, but so purely and sweetly now, in the arms of Faith! Amidst these pleasant and praiseworthy meditations, Goodman Brown heard the tramp of horses along the road, and deemed it advisable to conceal himself within the verge of the forest, conscious of the guilty purpose that had brought him thither, though now so happily turned from it.

On came the hoof tramps and the voices of the riders, two grave old voices, conversing soberly as they drew near. These mingled sounds appeared to pass along the road, within a few yards of the young man's hiding-place; but, owing doubtless to the depth of the gloom at that particular spot, neither the travelers nor their steeds were visible. Though their figures brushed the small boughs by the wayside, it could not be seen that they intercepted, even for a moment, the faint gleam from the strip of bright sky athwart which they must have passed. Goodman Brown alternately crouched and stood on tiptoe, pulling aside the branches and thrusting forth his head as far as he durst, without discerning so much as a shadow. It vexed him the more, because he could have sworn, were such a thing possible, that he recognized the voices of the minister and Deacon Gookin, jogging along quietly, as they were wont to do, when bound to some ordination or ecclesiastical council. While yet within hearing, one of the riders stopped to pluck a switch.

'Of the two, reverend sir,' said the voice like the deacon's, 'I had rather miss an ordination dinner than tonight's meeting. They tell me that some of our community are to be here from Falmouth and beyond, and others from Connecticut and Rhode Island, besides several of the Indian pow-wows, who, after their fashion, know almost as much deviltry as the best of us. Moreover, there is a goodly young woman to be taken into communion.'

'Mighty well, Deacon Gookin!' replied the solemn old tones of the minister. 'Spur up, or we shall be late. Nothing can be done, you know, until I get on the ground.'

The hoofs clattered again; and the voices, talking so strangely in the empty air, passed on through the forest, where no church had ever been gathered or solitary Christian prayed. Whither, then, could these holy men be journeying so deep into the heathen wilderness? Young Goodman Brown caught hold of a tree for support, being ready to sink down on the ground, faint and overburdened with the heavy sickness of his heart. He looked up to the sky, doubting whether there really was a heaven above him. Yet there was the blue arch, and the stars brightening in it.

'With heaven above and Faith below, I will yet stand firm against the Devil!' cried Goodman Brown.

While he still gazed upward into the deep arch of the firmament and had lifted his hands to pray, a cloud, though no wind was stirring, hurried across the zenith and hid the brightening stars. The blue sky was still visible, except directly overhead, where this black mass of cloud was sweeping swiftly northward.

Aloft in the air, as if from the depths of the cloud, came a confused and doubtful sound of voices. Once the listener fancied that he could distinguish the accents of townspeople of his own, men and women, both pious and ungodly, many of whom he had met at the communion table, and had seen others rioting at the tavern. The next moment, so indistinct were the sounds, he doubted whether he had heard aught but the murmur of the old forest, whispering without a wind. Then came a stronger swell of those familiar tones, heard daily in the sunshine at Salem village, but never until now from a cloud of night. There was one voice, of a young woman, uttering lamentations, yet with an uncertain sorrow, and entreating for some favor, which, perhaps, it would grieve her to obtain; and all the unseen multitude, both saints and sinners, seemed to encourage her onward.

'Faith!' shouted Goodman Brown, in a voice of agony and desperation; and the echoes of the forest mocked him, crying, 'Faith! Faith!' as if bewildered wretches were seeking her all through the wilderness.

The cry of grief, rage, and terror was yet piercing the night, when the unhappy husband held his breath for a response. There was a scream, drowned immediately in a louder murmur of voices, fading into far-off laughter, as the dark cloud swept away, leaving the clear and silent sky above Goodman Brown. But something fluttered lightly down through the air and caught on the branch of a tree. The young man seized it, and beheld a pink ribbon.

'My Faith is gone!' cried he, after one stupefied moment. 'There is no good on earth; and sin is but a name. Come, Devil; for to thee is this world given.'

And, maddened with despair, so that he laughed loud and long, did Goodman Brown grasp his staff and set forth again, at such a rate that he seemed to fly along the forest path rather than to walk or run. The road grew wilder and drearier and more faintly traced, and vanished at length, leaving him in the heart of the dark wilderness, still rushing onward with the instinct that guides mortal man to evil. The whole forest was peopled with frightful sounds – the creaking of the trees, the howling of wild beasts, and the yell of Indians; while sometimes the wind tolled like a distant church-bell, and sometimes gave a broad roar around the traveler, as if all Nature were laughing him to scorn. But he was himself the chief horror of the scene, and shrank not from its other horrors.

'Ha! ha! ha!' roared Goodman Brown when the wind laughed at him. 'Let us hear which will laugh loudest. Think not to frighten me with your deviltry. Come witch, come wizard, come Indian pow-wow, come Devil himself, and here comes Goodman Brown. You may as well fear him as he fear you.'

In truth, all through the haunted forest there could be nothing more frightful than the figure of Goodman Brown. On he flew among the black pines, brandishing his staff with frenzied gestures, now giving vent to an inspiration of horrid blasphemy, and now shouting forth such laughter as set all the echoes of the forest laughing like demons around him. The fiend in his own shape is less hideous than when he rages in the breast of man. Thus sped the demoniac on his course, until, quivering among the trees, he saw a red light before him, as when the felled trunks and branches of a clearing have been set on fire, and throw up their lurid blaze against the sky, at the hour of midnight. He paused, in a lull of the tempest that had driven him onward, and heard the swell of what seemed a hymn rolling solemnly from a distance with the weight of many voices. He knew the tune; it was a familiar one in the choir of the village meeting-house. The verse died heavily away, and was lengthened by a chorus, not of human voices, but of all the sounds of the benighted wilderness pealing in awful harmony together. Goodman Brown cried out, and his cry was lost to his own ear by its unison with the cry of the desert.

In the interval of silence he stole forward until the light glared full upon his eyes. At one extremity of an open space, hemmed in by the dark wall of the forest, arose a rock, bearing some rude, natural resemblance either to an altar or a pulpit, and surrounded by four blazing pines, their tops aflame, their stems untouched, like candles at an evening meeting. The mass of foliage that had overgrown the summit of the rock was all on fire, blazing high into the night and fitfully illuminating the whole field. Each pendent twig and leafy festoon was in a blaze. As the red light arose and fell, a numerous congregation alternately shone forth, then disappeared in shadow, and again grew, as it were, out of the darkness, peopling the heart of the solitary woods at once.

'A grave and dark-clad company,' quoth Goodman Brown.

Nathaniel Hawthorne, 'Young Goodman Brown' (1835)

A Famous Footprint

It happened one day, about noon, going towards my boat, I was exceedingly surprised with the print of a man's naked foot on the shore, which was very plain to see on the sand. I stood like one thunder struck, or as if I had seen an apparition. I listened, I looked round me, but I could hear nothing, nor see anything. I went up to a rising ground to look further. I went up the shore, and down the shore, but it was all one. I could see no other impression but that one. I went to it again to see if there were any more, and to observe it might not be my fancy, but there was no room for that, for there was exactly the print of a foot – toes, heel, and every part of a foot. How it came thither I knew not, nor could I in the least imagine. But after innumerable fluttering thoughts, like a man perfectly confused and out of myself, I came home to my fortification, not feeling, as we say, the ground I went on.

Daniel Defoe, *Robinson Crusoe* (1719)

Walking the Dog

The man flung a look back along the way he had come. The Yukon lay a mile wide and hidden under three feet of ice. On top of this ice were as many feet of snow. It was all pure white, rolling in gentle undulations where the ice-jams of the freeze-up had formed. North and south, as far as his eye could see, it was unbroken white, save for a dark hairline that curved and twisted from around the spruce-covered island to the south, and that curved and twisted away into the north, where it disappeared behind another spruce-covered island. This dark hairline was the trail – the main trail – that led south five hundred miles to the Chilcoot Pass, Dyea, and salt water; and led north seventy miles to Nulato, and finally to St Michael, on Bering Sea, a thousand miles and a half thousand more.

But all this – the mysterious, far-reaching hair-line trail, the absence of sun from the sky, the tremendous cold, and the strangeness and weirdness of it all – made no impression on the man. It was not because he was long used to it. He was a newcomer in the land, a *chechaquo*, and this was his first winter. The trouble with him was that he was without imagination. He was quick and alert in the things of life, but only in the things, and not in the significances. Fifty degrees below zero meant eighty-odd degrees of frost. Such fact impressed him as being cold and uncomfortable, and that was all... That there should be anything more to it than that was a thought that never entered his head.

As he turned to go on, he spat speculatively. There was a sharp, explosive crackle that startled him. He spat again. And again, in the air, before it could fall to the snow, the spittle crackled. He knew that at fifty below spittle crackled on the snow, but this spittle had crackled in the air. Undoubtedly it was colder than fifty below – how much colder he did not know. But the temperature did not matter. He was bound for the old claim on the left fork of Henderson Creek, where the boys were already… He would be in to camp by six o'clock; a bit after dark, it was true, but the boys would be there, a fire would be going, and a hot supper would be ready. As for lunch, he pressed his hand against the protruding bundle under his jacket. It was also under his shirt, wrapped up in a handkerchief and lying against the naked skin. It was the only way to keep the biscuits from freezing. He smiled agreeably to himself as he thought of those biscuits, each cut open and sopped in bacon grease, and each enclosing a generous slice of fried bacon.

He plunged in among the big spruce trees. The trail was faint. A foot of snow had fallen since the last sled had passed over, and he was glad he was without a sled, travelling light. In fact, he carried nothing but the lunch wrapped in the handkerchief. He was surprised, however, at the cold. It certainly was cold, he concluded, as he rubbed his numb nose and cheekbones with his mittened hand. He was a warm-whiskered man, but the hair on his face did not protect the high cheekbones and the eager nose that thrust itself aggressively into the frosty air.

At the man's heels trotted a dog, a big native husky, the proper wolf-dog, gray-coated and without any visible or temperamental difference from its brother, the wild wolf. The animal was depressed by the tremendous cold. It knew that it was no time for travelling… It experienced a vague but menacing apprehension that subdued it and made it slink along at the man's heels, and that made it question every unwonted movement of the man as if expecting him to go into camp or to seek shelter somewhere and build a fire. The dog had learned fire, and it wanted fire…

The man held on through the level stretch of woods for several miles… and dropped down a bank to the frozen bed of a small stream. This was Henderson Creek, and he knew he was ten miles from the forks. He looked at his watch. It was ten o'clock. He was making four miles an hour, and he calculated that he would arrive at the forks at half-past twelve. He decided to celebrate that event by eating his lunch there.

The dog dropped in again at his heels, with a tail drooping discouragement, as the man swung along the creek-bed... just then particularly he had nothing to think about save that he would eat lunch at the forks and that at six o'clock he would be in camp with the boys...

As he walked along he rubbed his cheekbones and nose with the back of his mittened hand. He did this automatically, now and again changing hands. But rub as he would, the instant he stopped his cheekbones went numb, and the following instant the end of his nose went numb...

Empty as the man's mind was of thoughts, he was keenly observant, and he noticed the changes in the creek, the curves and bends and timber-jams, and always he sharply noted where he placed his feet. Once, coming around a bend, he shied abruptly, like a startled horse, curved away from the place where he had been walking, and retreated several paces back along the trail. The creek he knew was frozen clear to the bottom – no creek could contain water in that arctic winter – but he knew also that there were springs that bubbled out from the hillsides and ran along under the snow and on top the ice of the creek. He knew that the coldest snaps never froze these springs, and he knew likewise their danger. They were traps. They hid pools of water under the snow that might be three inches deep, or three feet. Sometimes a skin of ice half an inch thick covered them, and in turn was covered by the snow. Sometimes there were alternate layers of water and ice-skin, so that when one broke through he kept on breaking through for a while, sometimes wetting himself to the waist.

That was why he had shied in such panic. He had felt the give under his feet and heard the crackle of a snow-hidden ice-skin. And to get his feet wet in such a temperature meant trouble and danger. At the very least it meant delay, for he would be forced to stop and build a fire, and under its protection to bare his feet while he dried his socks and moccasins. He stood and studied the creek-bed and its banks, and decided that the flow of water came from the right. He reflected awhile, rubbing his nose and cheeks, then skirted to the left, stepping gingerly and testing the footing for each step. Once clear of the danger, he took a fresh chew of tobacco and swung along at his four-mile gait...

He compelled the dog to go on in front. The dog did not want to go. It hung back until the man shoved it forward, and then it went quickly across the white, unbroken surface. Suddenly it broke through, floundered to one side, and got away to firmer footing. It had wet its forefeet and legs, and almost immediately the water that clung to it turned to ice. It made quick efforts to lick the ice off its legs, then dropped down in the snow and began to bite out the ice that had formed between the toes. This was a matter of instinct. To permit the ice to remain would mean sore feet. It did not know this. It merely obeyed the mysterious prompting that arose from the deep crypts of its being...

At twelve o'clock the day was at its brightest. Yet the sun was too far south on its winter journey to clear the horizon. The bulge of the earth intervened between it and Henderson Creek, where the man walked under a clear sky at noon and cast no shadow. At half-past twelve, to the minute, he arrived at the forks of the creek. He was pleased at the speed he had made. If he kept it up, he would certainly be with the boys by six. He unbuttoned his jacket and shirt and drew forth his lunch. The action consumed no more than a quarter of a minute, yet in that brief moment the numbness laid hold of the exposed fingers. He did not put the mitten on, but, instead, struck the fingers a dozen sharp smashes against his leg. Then he sat down on a snow-covered log to eat. The sting that followed upon the striking of his fingers against his leg ceased so quickly that he was startled. He had had no chance to take a bite of biscuit. He struck the fingers repeatedly and returned them to the mitten, baring the other hand for the purpose of eating. He tried to take a mouthful, but the ice-muzzle prevented. He had forgotten to build a fire and thaw out. He chuckled at his foolishness...

He pulled the mitten on hurriedly and stood up. He was a bit frightened. He stamped up and down until the stinging returned into the feet. It certainly was cold, was his thought... There was no mistake about it, it *was* cold. He strode up and down, stamping his feet and threshing his arms, until reassured by the returning warmth. Then he got out matches and proceeded to make a fire. From the undergrowth, where high water of the previous spring had lodged a supply of seasoned twigs, he got his firewood. Working carefully from a small beginning, he soon had a roaring fire, over which he thawed the ice from his face and in the protection of which he ate his biscuits. For the moment the cold of space was outwitted. The dog took satisfaction in the fire, stretching out close enough for warmth and far enough away to escape being singed.

When the man had finished, he filled his pipe and took his comfortable time over a smoke. Then he pulled on his mittens, settled the ear-flaps of his cap firmly about his ears, and took the creek trail up the left fork. The dog was disappointed and yearned back toward the fire...

There did not seem to be so many springs on the left fork of the Henderson, and for half an hour the man saw no signs of any. And then it happened. At a place where there were no signs, where the soft, unbroken snow seemed to advertise solidity beneath, the man broke through. It was not deep. He wet himself halfway to the knees before he floundered out to the firm crust.

He was angry, and cursed his luck aloud. He had hoped to get into camp with the boys at six o'clock, and this would delay him an hour, for he would have to build a fire and dry out his foot-gear. This was imperative at that low temperature – he knew that much; and he turned aside to the bank, which he climbed. On top, tangled in the underbrush about the trunks of several small spruce trees, was a high-water deposit of dry firewood – sticks and twigs...

He worked slowly and carefully, keenly aware of his danger...

Already all sensation had gone out of his feet. To build the fire he had been forced to remove his mittens, and the fingers had quickly gone numb. His pace of four miles an hour had kept his heart pumping blood to the surface of his body and to all the extremities. But the instant he stopped, the action of the pump eased down... The extremities were the first to feel its absence...

But he was safe. Toes and nose and cheeks would be only touched by the frost, for the fire was beginning to burn with strength... The fire was a success. He was safe...

He started to untie his moccasins. They were coated with ice; the thick German socks were like sheaths of iron halfway to the knees; and the moccasin strings were like rods of steels all twisted and knotted as by some conflagration. For a moment he tugged with his numb fingers, then, realizing the folly of it, he drew his sheath-knife.

But before he could cut the strings, it happened. It was his own fault or, rather, his mistake. He should not have built the fire under the spruce tree. He should have built it in the open... High up in the tree one bough capsized its load of snow. This fell on the boughs beneath, capsizing them. This process continued, spreading out and involving the whole tree. It grew like an avalanche, and it descended without warning upon the man and the fire, and the fire was blotted out! Where it had burned was a mantle of fresh and disordered snow.

The man was shocked... Then he grew very calm... it was up to him to build the fire over again, and this second time there must be no failure. Even if he succeeded, he would most likely lose some toes. His feet must be badly frozen by now, and there would be some time before the second fire was ready...

He made a new foundation for a fire, this time in the open, where no treacherous tree could blot it out. Next, he gathered dry grasses and tiny twigs from the high-water flotsam. He could not bring his fingers together to pull them out, but he was able to gather them by the handful. In this way he got many rotten twigs and bits of green moss that were undesirable, but it was the best he could do. He worked methodically, even collecting an armful of the larger branches to be used later when the fire gathered strength. And all the while the dog sat and watched him, a certain yearning wistfulness in its eyes, for it looked upon him as the fire-provider, and the fire was slow in coming.

When all was ready, the man reached in his pocket for a second piece of birch-bark. He knew the bark was there, and, though he could not feel it with his fingers, he could hear its crisp rustling as he fumbled for it. Try as he would, he could not clutch hold of it. And all the time, in his consciousness, was the knowledge that each instant his feet were freezing. This thought tended to put him in a panic, but he fought against it and kept calm. He pulled on his mittens with his teeth, and threshed his arms back and forth, beating his hands with all his might against his sides. He did this sitting down, and he stood up to do it; and all the while the dog sat in the snow, its wolf-brush of a tail curled around warmly over its forefeet, its sharp wolf-ears pricked forward intently as it watched the man. And the man, as he beat and threshed with his arms and hands, felt a great surge of envy as he regarded the creature that was warm and secure in its natural covering.

After a time he was aware of the first faraway signals of sensation in his beaten fingers. The faint tingling grew stronger till it evolved into a stinging ache that was excruciating, but which the man hailed with satisfaction. He stripped the mitten from his right hand and fetched forth the birch-bark. The exposed fingers were quickly going numb again. Next he brought out his bunch of sulphur matches. But the tremendous cold had already driven the life out of his fingers. In his effort to separate one match from the others, the whole bunch fell in the snow. He tried to pick it out of the snow, but failed. The dead fingers could neither touch nor clutch. He was very careful. He drove the thought of his freezing feet, and nose, and cheeks, out of his mind, devoting his whole soul to the matches. He watched, using the sense of vision in place of that of touch, and when he saw his fingers on each side the bunch, he closed them – that is, he willed to close them, for the wires were down, and the fingers did not obey. He pulled the mitten on the right hand, and beat it fiercely against his knee. Then, with both mittened hands, he scooped the bunch of matches, along with much snow, into his lap. Yet he was no better off.

After some manipulation he managed to get the bunch between the heels of his mittened hands. In this fashion he carried it to his mouth. The ice crackled and snapped when by a violent effort he opened his mouth. He drew the lower jaw in, curled the upper lip out of the way, and scraped the bunch with his upper teeth in order to separate a match. He succeeded in getting one, which he dropped on his lap. He was no better off. He could not pick it up. Then he devised a way. He picked it up in his teeth and scratched it on his leg. Twenty times he scratched before he succeeded in lighting it. As it flamed he held it with his teeth to the birch-bark. But the burning brimstone went up his nostrils and into his lungs, causing him to cough spasmodically. The match fell into the snow and went out.

That old-timer on Sulphur Creek was right, he thought in the moment of controlled despair that ensued: after fifty below, a man should travel with a partner. He beat his hands, but failed in exciting any sensation. Suddenly he bared both hands, removing the mittens with his teeth. He caught the whole bunch between the heels of his hands. His arm-muscles not being frozen enabled him to press the hand-heels tightly against the matches. Then he scratched the bunch along his leg. It flared into flame, seventy sulphur matches at once! There was no wind to blow them out. He kept his head to one side to escape the strangling fumes, and held the blazing bunch to the birch-bark. As he so held it, he became aware of sensation in his hand. His flesh was burning. He could smell it. Deep down below the surface he could feel it. The sensation developed into pain that grew acute. And still he endured it, holding the flame of the matches clumsily to the bark that would not light readily because his own burning hands were in the way, absorbing most of the flame.

At last, when he could endure no more, he jerked his hands apart. The blazing matches fell sizzling into the snow, but the birch-bark was alight. He began laying dry grasses and the tiniest twigs on the flame. He could not pick and choose, for he had to lift the fuel between the heels of his hands. Small pieces of rotten wood and green moss clung to the twigs, and he bit them off as well as he could with his teeth. He cherished the flame carefully and awkwardly. It meant life, and it must not perish. The withdrawal of blood from the surface of his body now made him begin to shiver, and he grew more awkward. A large piece of green moss fell squarely on the little fire. He tried to poke it out with his fingers, but his shivering frame made him poke too far, and he disrupted the nucleus of the little fire, the burning grasses and tiny twigs separating and scattering. He tried to poke them together again, but in spite of the tenseness of the effort, his shivering got away with him, and the twigs were hopelessly scattered. Each twig gushed a puff of smoke and went out. The fire-provider had failed. As he looked apathetically about him, his eyes chanced on the dog, sitting across the ruins of the fire from him, in the snow, making restless, hunching movements, slightly lifting one forefoot and then the other, shifting its weight back and forth on them with wistful eagerness.

The sight of the dog put a wild idea into his head. He remembered the tale of the man, caught in a blizzard, who killed a steer and crawled inside the carcass, and so was saved. He would kill the dog and bury his hands in the warm body until the numbness went out of them. Then he could build another fire. He spoke to the dog, calling it to him; but in his voice was a strange note of fear that frightened the animal, who had never known the man to speak in such way before. Something was the matter, and its suspicious nature sensed danger – it knew not what danger, but somewhere, somehow, in its brain arose an apprehension of the man. It flattened its ears down at the sound of the man's voice, and its restless, hunching movements and the liftings and shift-ings of its forefeet became more pronounced; but it would not come to the man. He got on his hands and knees and crawled toward the dog. This unusual posture again excited suspicion, and the animal sidled away.

The man sat up in the snow for a moment and struggled for calmness...

A certain fear of death, dull and oppressive, came to him. This fear quickly became poignant as he realized that it was no longer a mere matter of freezing his fingers and toes, or of losing his hands and feet, but that it was a matter of life and death with the chances against him. This threw him into a panic, and he turned and ran up the creek-bed along the old, dim trail. The dog joined in behind and kept up with him. He ran blindly, without intention, in fear such as he had never known in his life. Slowly, as he ploughed and floundered through the snow, he began to see things again, – the banks of the creek, the old timber-jams, the leafless aspens, and the sky. The running made him feel better. He did not shiver. Maybe, if he ran on, his feet would thaw out; and, anyway, if he ran far enough, he would reach camp and the boys. Without doubt he would lose some fingers and toes and some of his face; but the boys would take care of him, and save the rest of him when he got there...

Several times he stumbled, and finally he tottered, crumpled up, and fell. When he tried to rise, he failed. He must sit and rest, he decided, and next time he would merely walk and keep on going. As he sat and regained his breath, he noted that he was feeling quite warm and comfortable. He was not shivering, and it even seemed that a warm glow had come to his chest and trunk. And yet, when he touched his nose or cheeks, there was no sensation. Running would not thaw them out. Nor would it thaw out his hands and feet. Then the thought came to him that the frozen portions of his body must be extending...

The thought of it drove him on, but he ran no more than a hundred feet, when he staggered and pitched headlong. It was his last panic. When he had recovered his breath and control, he sat up and entertained in his mind the conception of meeting death with dignity. However, the conception did not come to him in such terms. His idea of it was that he had been making a fool of himself, running around like a chicken with its head cut off – such was the simile that occurred to him...

He pictured the boys finding his body next day. Suddenly he found himself with them, coming along the trail and looking for himself...

Then the man drowsed off into what seemed to him the most comfortable and satisfying sleep he had ever known. The dog sat facing him and waiting. The brief day drew to a close in a long, slow twilight. There were no signs of a fire to be made, and besides, never in the dog's experience had it known a man to sit like that in the snow and make no fire. As the twilight drew on, its eager yearning for the fire mastered it, and with a great lifting and shifting of forefeet, it whined softly, then flattened its ears down in anticipation of being chidden by the man. But the man remained silent. Later, the dog whined loudly. And still later it crept close to the man and caught the scent of death. This made the animal bristle and back away. A little longer it delayed, howling under the stars that leaped and danced and shone brightly in the cold sky. Then it turned and trotted up the trail in the direction of the camp it knew, where were the other food-providers and fire-providers.

Jack London, 'To Build a Fire' (1908)

Final Steps

Slowly the sun had climbed up the hard white downs, till it broke with little of the mysterious ritual of dawn upon a sparkling world of snow. There had been a hard frost during the night, and the birds, who hopped about here and there with scant tolerance of life, left no trace of their passage on the silver pavements. In places the sheltered caverns of the hedges broke the monotony of the whiteness that had fallen upon the coloured earth, and overhead the sky melted from orange to deep blue, from deep blue to a blue so pale that it suggested a thin paper screen rather than illimitable space. Across the level fields there came a cold, silent wind which blew a fine dust of snow from the trees, but hardly stirred the crested hedges. Once above the skyline, the sun seemed to climb more quickly, and as it rose higher it began to give out a heat that blended with the keenness of the wind.

It may have been this strange alternation of heat and cold that disturbed the tramp in his dreams, for he struggled for a moment with the snow that covered him, like a man who finds himself twisted uncomfortably in the bedclothes, and then sat up with staring, questioning eyes. 'Lord! I thought I was in bed,' he said to himself as he took in the vacant landscape, 'and all the while I was out here.' He stretched his limbs, and, rising carefully to his feet, shook the snow off his body. As he did so the wind set him shivering, and he knew that his bed had been warm.

'Come, I feel pretty fit,' he thought. 'I suppose I am lucky to wake at all in this. Or unlucky – it isn't much of a business to come back to.' He looked up and saw the downs shining against the blue like the Alps on a picture-postcard. 'That means another forty miles or so, I suppose,' he continued grimly. 'Lord knows what I did yesterday. Walked till I was done, and now I'm only about twelve miles from Brighton. Damn the snow, damn Brighton, damn everything!' The sun crept higher and higher, and he started walking patiently along the road with his back turned to the hills.

'Am I glad or sorry that it was only sleep that took me, glad or sorry, glad or sorry?' His thoughts seemed to arrange themselves in a metrical accompaniment to the steady thud of his footsteps, and he hardly sought an answer to his question. It was good enough to walk to.

Presently, when three milestones had loitered past, he overtook a boy who was stooping to light a cigarette. He wore no overcoat, and looked unspeakably fragile against the snow. 'Are you on the road, guv'nor?' asked the boy huskily as he passed.

'I think I am,' the tramp said.

'Oh! then I'll come a bit of the way with you if you don't walk too fast. It's bit lonesome walking this time of day.'

The tramp nodded his head, and the boy started limping along by his side.

'I'm eighteen,' he said casually. 'I bet you thought I was younger.'

'Fifteen, I'd have said.'

'You'd have backed a loser. Eighteen last August, and I've been on the road six years. I ran away from home five times when I was a little 'un, and the police took me back each time. Very good to me, the police was. Now I haven't got a home to run away from.'

'Nor have I,' the tramp said calmly.

'Oh, I can see what you are,' the boy panted; 'you're a gentleman come down. It's harder for you than for me.' The tramp glanced at the limping, feeble figure and lessened his pace.

'I haven't been at it as long as you have,' he admitted.

'No, I could tell that by the way you walk. You haven't got tired yet. Perhaps you expect something at the other end?'

The tramp reflected for a moment. 'I don't know,' he said bitterly, 'I'm always expecting things.'

'You'll grow out of that,' the boy commented. 'It's warmer in London, but it's harder to come by grub. There isn't much in it really.'

'Still, there's the chance of meeting somebody there who will understand –'

'Country people are better,' the boy interrupted. 'Last night I took a lease of a barn for nothing and slept with the cows, and this morning the farmer routed me out and gave me tea and toke because I was so little. Of course, I score there; but in London, soup on the Embankment at night, and all the rest of the time coppers moving you on.'

'I dropped by the roadside last night and slept where I fell. It's a wonder I didn't die,' the tramp said. The boy looked at him sharply.

'How do you know you didn't?' he said.

'I don't see it,' the tramp said, after a pause.

'I tell you,' the boy said hoarsely, 'people like us can't get away from this sort of thing if we want to. Always hungry and thirsty and dog-tired and walking all the while. And yet if anyone offers me a nice home and work my stomach feels sick. Do I look strong? I know I'm little for my age, but I've been knocking about like this for six years, and do you think I'm not dead? I was drowned bathing at Margate, and I was killed by a gipsy with a spike; he knocked my head right in, and twice I was froze like you last night, and a motor cut me down on this very road, and yet I'm walking along here now, walking to London to walk away from it again, because I can't help it. Dead! I tell you we can't get away if we want to.'

The boy broke off in a fit of coughing, and the tramp paused while he recovered.

'You'd better borrow my coat for a bit, Tommy,' he said, 'your cough's pretty bad.'

'You go to hell!' the boy said fiercely, puffing at his cigarette; 'I'm all right. I was telling you about the road. You haven't got down to it yet, but you'll find out presently. We're all dead, all of us who're on it, and we're all tired, yet somehow we can't leave it. There's nice smells in the summer, dust and hay and the wind smack in your face on a hot day – and it's nice waking up in the wet grass on a fine morning. I don't know, I don't know –' he lurched forward suddenly, and the tramp caught him in his arms.

'I'm sick,' the boy whispered, 'sick.'

The tramp looked up and down the road, but he could see no houses or any sign of help. Yet even as he supported the boy doubtfully in the middle of the road a motorcar suddenly flashed in the middle distance, and came smoothly through the snow.

'What's the trouble?' said the driver quietly as he pulled up. 'I'm a doctor.' He looked at the boy keenly and listened to his strained breathing. 'Pneumonia,' he commented. 'I'll give him a lift to the infirmary, and you, too, if you like.'

The tramp thought of the workhouse and shook his head. 'I'd rather walk,' he said.

The boy winked faintly as they lifted him into the car.

'I'll meet you beyond Reigate,' he murmured to the tramp. 'You'll see.' And the car vanished along the white road.

All the morning the tramp splashed through the thawing snow, but at midday he begged some bread at a cottage door and crept into a lonely barn to eat it. It was warm in there, and after his meal he fell asleep among the hay. It was dark when he woke, and started trudging once more through the slushy roads.

Two miles beyond Reigate a figure, a fragile figure, slipped out of the darkness to meet him.

'On the road, guv'nor?' said a husky voice. 'Then I'll come a bit of the way with you if you don't walk too fast. It's a bit lonesome walking this time of day.'

'But the pneumonia!' cried the tramp, aghast.

'I died at Crawley this morning,' said the boy.

Richard Middleton, *On The Brighton Road* (1912)

Walk on…

'Now let us walk,' muttered the lama, and to the click of his rosary walked in silence mile upon mile. The lama, as usual, was deep in meditation, but Kim's bright eyes were open wide. This broad, smiling river of life, he considered, was a vast improvement on the cramped and crowded Lahore streets. There were new people and new streets at every stride…

From time to time the lama took snuff, and at last Kim could endure the silence no longer.

'This is a good land – the land of the South!' said he. 'The air is good, the water is good. Eh?'

'And they are all bound upon the Wheel,' said the lama. 'Bound from life after life. To none of these has the Way been shown.' He shook himself back to this world.

Rudyard Kipling, *Kim* (1901)

It has been a delightful journey, this journey home.
I have walked on foot.
Olive Schreiner

Acknowledgements

Walking might have its solitary side but publishing a book on the subject will always involve others. So I would like to thank Rachel Calder, Polly Card, Martha Pooley, Ellie Robins and Will Self for their help in putting these pages together.

The editor and publishers acknowledge permission to reprint material from the following:

'A Sudden Walk' from *Metamorphosis and Other Stories* by Franz Kafka, translated by Michael Hoffman 2007, by permission of Pengiun US/UK; *A Journey Around My Room* by Xavier De Maistre, translated by Andrew Brown 2004, Hesperus Press; 'Bed 29' from *A Day In The Country And Other Stories* by Guy De Maupassant, translated by David Coward 1990, by permission of Oxford University Press; *Notes from the Underground* by Fyodor Dostoevsky, translated by Hugh Aplin 2006, Hesperus Press.

Biographical note

Duncan Minshull is a producer at BBC Radio and the editor of various anthologies, including *The Vintage Book of Walking*. He has also written about the subject of walking for newspapers and magazines. He lives in west London.